Günter von Hummel

Outsmarting Death two Times

Life in Dying, a Treatise on Sisyphus and on a
New Self-Practice.

The cover image shows Sisyphus depicted on an antique Greek vase. One can see what heavy stone he has to drag up a hill. But the stone is not so much a stone of punishment, but more a stone of the into Sisyphus' soul primordial repressed. It is a stone of his addictions and desires as they still play a decisive role in the life of man today.

Production and Publishing
BoD, Books on Demand, Norderstedt
Germany
ISBN 9783753478753

Table of Contents

1. Introduction

In the middle of the last century, the Japanese writer Yasushi Inoue wrote a story about a man and a woman who met by chance in a secluded hotel by the sea without knowing that they both had the same intention: to leave life in tranquility. Since his book is called Shi to koi to nami, in English 'love', one certainly suspects immediately that the two will fall in love and not do what they intend. If the fact of such a meeting - they are the only guests of the hotel - is already quite artificial and not very plausible, the end of the story seems to me even more curious and almost perverse. The two protagonists come closer to each other only in a very bumpy way, but whether there is really love involved is never quite clear, although this is the firm intention of the author, which is characterized by traditional idealism.

Already on the first evening the two know about their identical motives and leave this coldly stay in the room. Even after the unsuccessful suicide of the woman - by drowning in the sea - on the day after they met, both continue to hold on to their intentions and only talk past each other. However, in return for the fact that the man helped her with a few things and words after the mishap of survival, she gives herself to him the following night - without any love, only in return, as she says. But when he then wants to jump from the cliff into the raging sea the following night, she had secretly followed him and says that she does not want to hold him back. However, if he jumps, she will also jump and die. Either way, live or die, nothing matters to her. And thus he cannot realize his decision to kill himself, because he would then, in addition, cause her death, also committing murder, so to speak.

The author does not use this argument, but in my opinion it is clear that not only love, but also blackmail is involved: "if you kill yourself, I will kill myself too". In this last conversation, the woman confronts the man with the irrelevance of his desire to kill, because his motive is that he has been 'dishonored'. While the woman's suicide decision was caused by lovesickness, the man's was caused by self-inflicted high losses of money and the danger of criminal prosecution for bribery. In Japan, bankers still throw themselves out of their skyscrapers after bankruptcies because of such 'dishonors', which is rather not the case with us in the western area. In our country, people kill themselves because of deep depression, severe abandonment or hopeless life circumstances.

"I will try to live", the man thinks to himself in the end, even if it is not said why, because still there is no talk of great love. It didn't have to be said, but one senses in the author the intention of the ethical construct, the samurai ideal, the traditionalist calculation, that it should be about a very special, dramatically originated and high-quality love, which is supposed to dissuade the two protagonists from their intention - after the infinitely curious coincidence of their meeting - in a rather blackmailing and almost perverse way. Finally, they let go of their plans only in the sense of a mutual zero-round: if he wants to end his life because of this 'dishonor', he should do it, she does not hold him back - she says - just as he would not have held her back the day before. Like you me, like me you - without further explanations.

Because of this, because the story seemed so transparent to me, I thought its blackmailing and sober ending was a little perverse. Yasushi Inoue should have written the story differently; for example, he could have put more binding words in the woman's mouth and let her say to the man: "Give us one more day to be able to talk about our relationship. Then decide whether you want to jump or not". After that, Inoue could have written about all the difficulties that existed with the two of them - betrayal of love on the part of the woman, total bankruptcy and breach of law on the part of the man - and then continued to ponder about what kind of love exists at all, how it could be lived out, and why it must come across to the reader in no other way than as so noble and so holy.

One could also put it this way: as in general, besides living and dying, regressing, falling back into earlier psycho-physical states, the return to the beginning as such, also plays the decisive role in this story. It is not at all about love (of whatever kind), it is about a hold, regaining of an alleged primordial trust, by more than X or Y (I choose these letters because they represent at the same time the sex chromosomes, man XY, woman XX, which are so important). Because in the movement and in the completely soundless primal scream in which both tear each other back from death, they also abuse each other as living. They live now only as a credit drawn on death, which they will one day have to repay. Oh God, life is bleak and love is difficult!

The same problem is also the subject of the film 'Love' by director M. Haneke, which was universally praised and received many awards. In the very old couple shown, the wife suffers a stroke and becomes increasingly demented. The husband cares for her devotedly, with great commitment and imagination, but towards the end of this empathetic drama, after still speaking to her confidentially, he smothers her with a pillow and lays her in bed draped with flowers. So again, throughout the film, something is conjured up that is supposed to be quite deep love, perfectly empathic in terms of everyday psychology and with a supposedly wonderful outcome, because the man hears her even after her death and also sees himself leaving the house with her, and so on.

But I don't know if it's better to say that the story ends tragically or even with a murder? Because maybe the caring man was just a narcissist who only got into the role of the optimal, comprehensively empathetic helper and in the end has to let out the true feelings: Destructiveness, coldness, murder. Because why didn't he talk to her before about how to arrange the end of life, maybe she would have preferred a more gentle and professional euthanasia. Because simply pressing a pillow on her, putting her in terrible suffocation, still feeling her defiant wriggling and other things cannot be an act of love. But this is exactly what the director tries to suggest, and most people believe him.

Because 'spiritually' she was already no longer there, also physically no longer healthy, and so it is assumed that it had been her own, intense wish to be redeemed anyway. But what is she being released from? People with dementia no longer really and painfully realize their departure from social life, their loss of memory, their apparent monotony, while it affects their environment, their relatives, much more and they suffer much more from the inaccessibility of the dementia patient than the patient himself. After all, the amount of care required is becoming ever greater, and if one wants to do everything alone, it is also excessively demanding and somehow pointless. Isn't it the man who finally goes crazy, doesn't know what to do, and thus finally kills his wife under the pretext of a good deed? Shouldn't the title of the book and the firm be 'Love', but 'The Deepfakes of Love'?

The film is perverse and whitewashes the aggression and hatred smoldering in the background with almost religious whitewashing. If narcissism, hatred or ignorance, the usual downsides of love, had been more openly in play, the whole film might have become a melodramatic tearjerker. For this would require great, deep-psychological and dramatically skillful narrative art, which is not in sight here. But this way the film - completely hiding everything abysmal - becomes a great romanticized success and moves the masses. As in Yasushi Inoue's story, pathos and ethos are not emphasized or clearly named, but rather these terms are supposed to arise in the reader or viewer - by themselves, as it were, from behind: thought or felt or even heard with devotion. The pillow, the murder tool, should thus be nothing else than the seal, than the heraldic love sign, in any case nothing unkind. How it goes on with the man then, cannot be shown any more, but must be embezzled.

For in order to conceal this embezzlement, the man subsequently has hallucinations of his dead wife, which are concealed fantasies of guilt, as they often occur with murderers and murderesses (e.g. Clytemnestra). In reality, he would have had to appear desperate or crazy, even if the excessive love and embellished empathy had actually taken place and could have been shown at least somehow bindingly. Even without having to recognize narcissism and murder guilt at such an advanced age, it would have been only half the truth and would have turned the film into a grotesque. Love lies; sure, that's the big topic today.

Can't it all be done completely differently? Can't you invent it (the combination of death, life, love, etc.) creatively, freely, big, lustful and strong? No, nonsense, all just inflated vocabulary. There must be - instead of all this chatter and talk - a dying and regressing in constructive form, in which one ends up neither dead, nor near dead, nor mad, nor in love delusion, nor otherwise aberrant. The matter does not have to be deadly serious, but it does have to be serious. I want to write about this and describe a procedure which - scientifically justified - provides a clear way out, a clear X-and-Y and a love also for the negative in itself. Thousands of people have already done this, they will say with a wink.

Well, then first a story that will not be boring, as the two stories (Inoue's story and Haneke's book and film) certainly are not. I use the reports about the old Greek heroes, for example the saga of Sisyphus (and a little bit also that of Prometheus), in that with them the plump and lustful heroic life is ruined by the wanton and ruthless goings-on of the gods, love comes along anyway only death-bearing and everything already has a perverse touch from the beginning (so it is quite modern?). But it will not contain a love lie.

Admittedly, it's exclusively male gods who are afflicting Sisyphus, thus only XYs. Couldn't one have written about a goddess, who indeed seeks the heroic man's life, but then the narrative ends in a love, which - without having to interpose an equal opportunities officer between man and goddess - ends in a regressive, regressive, procedure, which connects both beyond XY/XX? Anyway, I want to stick to the historical antecedents and their interpretations and offer a serious, scientific tract, a guide to Sisyphus and to a self-practical, self-analytical procedure developed from it. Above all, I want to write about life in death, that is, about life not after but in death, insofar as it has not yet died completely. Whether and which love, which life and death are involved, will then be secured for each one to decide for himself.

That Sisyphus stands not only for the agony of constantly rolling a boulder up a hill, but also for having twice cheated death, is known to very few. It is even less known that one can learn something from him in this respect for today. In our modern times, people believe that death can be cheated, outsmarted, especially with the help of highly developed medical technology and specialized medicines, and that life can thus be prolonged a little further. But this calculation is not entirely correct. For one thing, the drugs are not as great as one imagines when reading generalized reports about them. Certainly, Janus kinase inhibitors, for example, have enormously improved the treatment of myeloid leukaemia and similar diseases, and biologicals for rheumatism have also brought benefits, albeit increased side effects.

The situation is not so good with the new and highly praised checkpoint inhibitors and CAT cells, which are effective against certain cancers. Over 90% side effects are reported, some of them severe, and deaths have also been related. Often, new, high-profile cancer drugs extend life by only a few months, and the benefit is only external, as quality of life is usually worsened. On the other hand, people make far too little use of the possibilities of not only extending life externally with these disadvantages to the quality of life, but increasing life internally and elevating it to its proper purpose. Because the biological vita is only one side, always people have already strived for the true, in fact, in principle life, which goes far beyond the mere vita. Why prolong the bad life when there is another, good one?

I don't mean mystical, esoteric, religious and otherwise cultic approaches to keeping death at bay or even suppressing it altogether and invoking love sky-high, as Yasushi Inoue does. In doing so, I appreciate his books and his Buddhist- and Confucian-inclined way of life, with which he has been a role model for many readers. However, in this book I will stick to the science as it was developed by the French psychoanalyst J. Lacan.[1] I take his psychoanalysis as a starting point and also bring - inspired by Yasushi Inoue - meditative aspects into play in my explanations, which shall ultimately culminate in the description of the announced self-practice (an expression of the philosopher M. Foucault).

In the middle of the last century, the physician and psychologist Carl Albrecht designed a rationally critical method of self-analysis and practiced it for years in a self-interpreting way, which was still attached to mysticism, but can nevertheless already be declared as rational. He practiced the procedure of 'listening into oneself' by switching off everyday thoughts and concentrating on a concept coming from within and exclusively word-related.[2] Thus, an already solid and more or less ethically significant, literal expression should come to light

---

[1] It is neither a natural nor a spiritual science. Based on mathematics, Lacan called it a conjectural science. Conjecture means assumption, one proceeds from one well-founded assumption to the next until the last certainty is found.

[2] Albrecht, C., Das Mystische Wort (The mystical Word) (1951) S. 185

from within. Albrecht tried at the same time to examine rationally these words coming to him, in order to be able to give them a 'real' and profound valuation in a holistic and ethical direction.

In C. Albrecht's technique of a contemplative listening into himself to the mystical word coming from within, one senses immediately, however, that through the 'mystically arriving words' not a really new, real knowledge imposes itself upon him, but that it is a knowledge which he - Freud would say: in the preconscious - already has. The 'mystical' inspirations namely work like poems, which always have something darkly sublime about them like "Heart", or "Oh stone", "Light"! Albrecht's words repeat a firm patheticness and also awaken memories of the old German, of something that he already knows from somewhere, e.g. from theosophical poetry or religious allusions. He chooses something, he doesn't let the actually unconscious come to speak, he is already too conscious in his knowledge that his 'arriving words' will contain something elegant and then he only speaks this out. He lacks the Freudian or also the Socratic Eros, he represses something, something in him does not dare to make more daring assertions, and so his Daimonion (Sokrate's inner voice) sounds like religious poetry.

A really concrete or even bold statement, a knowledge from the unconscious that would be new, startling or apt, because aiming at Plato's 'divine madness' or at something that could be passed on to people as new, revolutionary, does not come about in Albrecht. It is like with many 'meditative' methods, where the medium gets the message only from the already familiar preconscious, not really from the unconscious, the inner transcendent. Why should a message from the unconscious make use of our ready-made language, is it not more obvious that it sounds incomprehensible at first, and we have to decipher it first? Shouldn't it sound like a foreign language? Nevertheless, Albrecht's attempt was courageous and interesting.

Although not directly now, I have continued in his footsteps in a similar way, trying to proceed in a more scientific, modern and psychoanalytic way. My method of *Analytic Psychocatharsis* consists of two exercises, of which only the second one contains this listening into oneself. I will not explain this method here again in all details. Only this much: the listening in is already preformed in a "linguistic-crystalline" (an expression of J. Lacan for the unconscious) form by the first exercise, in which a liberating, cathartic experience occurs. Namely, *formulaic word formations* are meditated upon, which contain several meanings in a single lettering, so that one cannot commit oneself to any of these meanings during meditative repetition and must remain with the pure - sometimes seemingly nonsensical - basic formulation. So, although they consist of clear language (linguistic), no meaning can be extracted, and so, these *formula-words* concentrate and narrow down everything linguistic to a minimum (crystalline).

This, however, strongly promotes contemplation in a direction analogous to psychoanalysis. One becomes free of disturbing thoughts and emotions, so that thus a form of catharsis, of liberating relaxation occurs. If one then concentrates in the second exercise on 'listening in', e.g. only on an inner tone, word-related 'phrases' occur, which have to do directly with the unconscious. I say 'phrases' because here too, as concerning the unconscious, Lacan spoke of so-called "ultra-reduced phrases". Also with Albrecht - apart from the unscientific methodology - the 'mystical words' coming to him were concise and ultra-reduced. The unconscious knows no usual syntax or grammar, but its statements have picture and language character (crystalline-linguistic), if necessary one must rationally touch up like even Albrecht did this.

Mostly, however, these "ultra-reduced phrases" are as Freud also claimed of some dreams: "as if freely read off the page".[3] Freud reports here of a dream in which the phrase "erzephilic" occurred. The dreamer himself immediately had the idea that the words "erzieherisch" (educational) and "syphilis" are contained in it, behind which a conflict of the dreamer was clearly hidden.[4] Written under each other, one notices that these broken dream letters are something where word-sound images

---

[3] Freud, S., GW Band II, Fischer (1999) S. 308.

[4] The dreamer had given a book with the title 'On Prostitution' to a woman in the evening in order to have an 'educational' effect on her, but then had the feeling himself that this might have had a 'poisoning' effect (like syphilis) on her.

```
erz  e  phil is  ch
erz  ie her  is  ch
     Sy phil is
```

intertwine like in the Freudian slip of the tongue. In the process, another word, whose meaning was displaced, inserts itself into the consciously uttered word, i.e. into its word-sound-character, whereby a completely different statement comes about than what one is conscious of.

The disguise by the inserted repressed was here easy to recognize for the dreamer, however Freud writes nothing to it, which was the actual problem of the dreamer. After all, one does not give a book about prostitution to a woman so un-self-consciously and then also immediately think of syphilis (as noted in footnote 4). But anyway, also in meditation it is not the repression but the shifting that is more in the foreground, which is visible in Albrecht's method. He simply shifts everything into the consciously elegant and pathetic. This is not the case with *Analytic Psychocatharsis*, which squeezes between repression and displacement and shifts unconscious content toward the "ultra-reduced phrases" that have to do with the identity of the subject. For the sake of simplicity, I will mention an example from my own experience in the very next chapter.

But first again a hint, why I spoke of life in the midst of death, thus of a condition, which is seen from the outside as end of life and with electroencephalography and magnetic resonance technology also scientifically precisely can be determined, but from the inside looks completely different. This is not only claimed by many mystics or myth tellers, I will also quote neuroscientists and give psychoanalytical arguments how in the transition from life to a very last death still other such regressive processes have meaning in the dying process. Because so said dying cannot only be learned, as one can often hear from esotericists, but its psychic structure can be experienced already long before.

2. What does Sisyphus offer?

"What does Sisyphus offer"? Was once the phrase emerging from the unconscious and so half aloud thought or shall one better say heard by me in the meditation. It was immediately clear to me that I myself was meant and that the *pass-word* (that's what I call these phrases that emerge from the unconscious as a result of my procedure) referred to my situation in several respects. On the one hand, I was Sisyphus, because I wrote book after book, gave lectures, and also organized a few seminars, but the response was moderate. I had done many psychoanalytic therapies and had hardly found anyone to whom I could recommend *Analytic Psychocatharsis*. Because people come to psychoanalytic therapy, which is recognized by the health insurance companies. But also because they want to talk, and to tell them to stay at home, do meditative exercises and we will discuss this from time to time, nobody wanted to hear.

Even in the lectures, to which often thirty to forty people came, only occasionally someone was found who wanted to learn the method, and most of those who had nevertheless read a book of mine found it interesting, but did not implement the method recommended in it. So I was a bit like Sisyphus with his hard work without success. I admit that the mentioned *formula-words* often sound strange, they often stimulated distortions, i.e. reactions which are also known from psychoanalysis and which

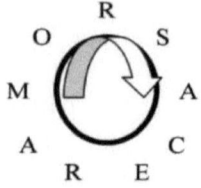

are called 'resistance' there; 'resistance' against the truth to be uncovered from the unconscious. Against the *formula-word*, for example, whose meaning I will explain later, a listener turned with the remark that he always hears the word 'marble sauce' (Marmor-Sosse) instead of the book sequence O.R.S.A.C.E.R.A.M. The word is written in a circle as it is shown in the picture above). Really mean, then, it had been very laborious to find formulations which, like this one from the Latin language, express several meanings, depending on the letter from which one begins to read.[5] The method was generally considered interesting and intellectually captivating, but perhaps for that very reason provoked the aforementioned resistance.

So I felt like Sisyphus, and this realization alone produced in me a new indifference: after all, I don't have to roll the stone of my texts up the mountain every day as Sisyphus had to do. If the thing is good, it will prevail, I thought to myself. And so that this really happens, I write this book, which I believe is the most understanda-

---

[5] For the provisional understanding here already once three of the readings: CERA MORSA, bitten wax, AMOR SACER, the love holy, MORS ACER, the death bitter, ERAM ORSA C, I was hundredfold intention. Even if some of them are nonsensical, it is important that all of them together do not make a unified sense and thus leave it to the unconscious. Further readings and additions to the procedure to it later.

ble of all the books I have written so far. For admittedly, I can be accused that my texts are not entirely easy to read. But it is about something that is scientifically well-founded and new, and at the same time represents a procedure derived from psychoanalysis and yet a procedure to be practiced meditatively by oneself at home.

As I will show, psychoanalysis and mediation are not contradictory. The very fact that in psychoanalysis the therapist should listen to his patient with "equal attention" - as Freud said - while the patient should express himself "freely associating" shows that both require an almost trance-like, meditative attitude. Thus, also with regard to "What does Sisyphus offer?", I felt as if a control analyst were asking me, using Sisyphus as a symbol of the unconscious, and by being me in meditation at the same time. It would not have helped me at all if someone had advised me not to take on writing and lecturing as Sisyphus did with his stone.

I would have taken note of that. But an 'inner sentence', which comes to one so personally and, in addition, seems so psychoanalytically enigmatically wise, is taken seriously. Never will the effect on the life of the soul be as strong as when it comes from one's own inner being and is also intellectually plausible. On the other hand, this *pass-word* contained another meaning. For it did not only mean "poor Sisyphus", "what does Sisyphus offer or mean", but what does this mythological type offer! What does this myth offer, does it perhaps not only consist in the old-known drudgery to which a sadistic god has condemned him? Or does he rather represent a role model in dealing with death that has lasted for generations? Because the myth offers more than just the heavy lifting.

So is he not only the prime example of the compulsively working man who must constantly drag the burden of life, the mighty stone, upwards where it falls down again into the valley. Doesn't his offer sound like a strange twisting of the myth, as, by the way, Camus also once declared. Camus wrote in his book 'The Myth of Sisyphus' that one "must imagine Sisyphus as a happy man". He related this - quasi somewhat antimarxistically - to the self-determination of the worker. The worker should say to himself, I do my part, my thing, in return I can determine myself in every other direction. The myth of Sisyphus was thus an offer to Camus to work out a philosophy of self-determination, even if it sounds somewhat paradoxical.

What Sisyphus can offer me, or I as a present-day Sisyphus, is not only about this *pass-word* as an example of existential interpretation. I also found in it the connection between the conscious and the unconscious. What was completely unconscious was the beginning of the *pass-word* with the "What does Sisyphus offer . „. For I had not dealt with this figure for ages (so it must have been buried in the extreme depths of my unconscious). I knew that I was probably overextending myself a bit with my writing, but the name Sisyphus would not have occurred to me. But the "offer" sounded like more and already coming from the preconscious. Such a small linking element does not disturb the message from the unconscious containing truth aspects, which consisted in the fact that I was Sisyphus, namely with regard to an offer. Now I do not offer that one has to imagine oneself as a happy person just like that, but I offer to outwit, outsmart death. That's another aspect that occurred to me by the myth.

You see, the historical Sisyphus was king of Corinth and failed not only in his adventures but also in women, which ultimately forced him to cheat death twice. He couldn't help but love women in numbers, albeit sometimes with a bit of violence. Moreover, when one day - in order to be given his own ever-bubbling, 'eternal' spring for his royal land holdings - he revealed to the river god Asopos that Zeus had kidnapped the latter's daughter Aigina, Zeus sent him the god Thanatos, Death, in revenge. After all, it had been about the disclosure of divine secrets, even Zeus' naughty deeds were under data protection! But Sisyphus managed to outwit Thanatos.

He first let him show him how to tie up the deceased in the underworld, so that they would not be able to get out of there, but then he tied him up himself in a flash according to his method. Some said that Sisyphus got Death drunk at first so that he could then put the shackles on him. Anyway, the trick worked and Thanatos was in any case no longer able to do anything, so no man could die. Only the god of war Ares freed Thanatos, because no more fighters would have died on the battle-fields, and nothing was worse for Ares than that! Even criminals, whose heads had been cut off, remained alive. Crazy! But Sisyphus cheated death a second time.

After Thanatos was freed, Sisyphus was sent to the realm of the dead again by Zeus. But even before he descended to Hades, the underworld, Sisyphus instructed his wife Merope not to bury him or perform any funeral rites. If one does not take death seriously, does nothing for a burial, even totally ignores this, it does not exist anymore; at least this was the motto at that time. Sisyphus immediately went to Persephone, the wife of Thanatos, who was much more empathetic than her husband, and explained to her that it was not at all in order to keep him here in Tartarus, in Hades. He must be allowed to return to the upper world, he demanded, claiming that he would be back in three days. Persephone gave in, but Sisyphus broke this promise and lived lustfully "many years" - as Camus writes - "at the bay of the gulf, on the shining sea, on the smiling earth" in his Corinthian kingdom. He enjoyed himself again with wife and children and perhaps also with another beloved, until finally Hermes, at the behest of Zeus, this humourless god, took him back down to Hades.

There, Sisyphus, the cunning and great hero, was condemned to this terrible act of having to roll a large stone over and over again up the mountain, or hill, from which it rolled back down before coming to rest at the very top. Perhaps one must see this not as punishment, but rather as a safety measure, so that he could not cheat death a third time. Labor procurement to regulate life were also known in ancient Greece. However, there are also indications that this whole story has rather to do with the sun titan, who always has to lift the heavy sun disk into the zenith, from where it then always rolls down again slowly into the night.[6] The myths of that time often intermingled, and so the doing of Sisyphus would be nothing else than an occupation to keep the world in its ups and downs, in its heights and depths.

Seen in this way, Sisyphus was indeed not a happy man, but a natural phenomenon that makes life on earth possible. Still in addition his father-in-law, thus Meropes producer, was the Titan Atlas who also already held such a world-preserving function: namely he had to carry the vault of heaven forever on his shoulders. Still long before Newton and Einstein he had recognized that it needs significant support for the ways of the planets and the sun. Thus the story of Sisyphus in a little bit projects into the old creation myths and have been mixed with later, sobering, bourgeois-secular narratives. So Sisyphus was at least a significant figure. Such a person, an important

---

[6] Ranke-Graves, von, R., Griechische Mythologie (Greec Mythology), Rowohlt (1974) Bd. II. S. 26

Corinthian king and world preserver were often elevated to gods as was the case with Heracles, for example. Sisyphus did not ascend to Olympus, he was simply too cunning and too sly. His rival on the throne Salmoneus, for example, he accused mendaciously of inbreeding and murder and thus had him deported out of the country.

But perhaps he can be considered a hero, just as today even mafia bosses are honored, who, precisely because they live in the underworld like Sisyphus, are also compared to heroes. As such, Sisyphus did not have to do easy work, but he was not really dead, because he who is really dead cannot work. Like Eros, he was a being between god and man, an interplay that was often the case with the ancient Greeks anyway. Even Homer called Sisyphus the most special and "cleverest (κέρδιστος) of men", and that is saying something![7] Homer was not a eulogist, he portrayed Sisyphus as a hero of high lineage, to which the warrior Glaucus explicitly referred in the Iliad.

Albert Camus portrays Sisyphus in his book 'The Myth of Sisyphus' as the hero of the absurd.[8] For Camus, the absurd was the decisive turning point that every thoughtful person must encounter at some point and then realize that life is worthwhile in spite of it, indeed precisely

---

[7] Homer, Ilias, Heimeran Publishing (1980) 6. Gesang, 153

[8] Camus, A., Der Mythos des Sisyphos (The Myth of Sisyphos), Rowohlt (2018) S. 141-147

because of it. Camus is interested in Sisyphus with regard to the moments on the way back from the mountain when the hero becomes aware of his tragedy and yet breathes a sigh of relief because he feels that, recognizing the absurd in its ridiculousness. "He is superior to his fate. He is stronger than his rock", Camus writes. And so I would like to present Sisyphus not exactly as a figure of light, but nevertheless as a bloody, life-strong role model from whom one can learn to outsmart death not only once, but several times, because such a thing - not only to overcome the absurd - is fundamentally necessary.

A little bit I actually think that my method of *Analytic Psychocatharsis* could contribute to helping people to outsmart death. For just as Sisyphus borrowed from himself the trick of outwitting Thanatos, so I borrowed from Lacan the essence of the *formula-words* that are at the heart of my procedure. I have already written of the "linguistic crystal" as Lacan's definition for the unconscious, in which the pictorial and the verbal combine most closely. This is also what is meant by the "défiles signifiantes", by the constrictions of the signifiers, of which Lacan constantly spoke, and which can be found in the constriction of the linguistic and pictorial sense of the *formula-words*.

In exaggerated terms, this means that everything that happens must pass through a bottleneck that is probably best defined by knowledge of the nature of death. Even the most sophisticated speech shows this phenomenon, in which politicians, experts and even lawyers constantly talk past each other. Real, mature information hardly gets through. Historians say that nothing is learned from history because it can never be recounted in the way that would be necessary for a reasonably accurate version. And that it is just as inaccurate in the realm of the imaginary, one does not need to prove any more. The bottleneck of imprecision, indeterminacy, and fake news crisscrosses contemporary life.

Through the many meanings in the *formula-word*, it comes about in a reversed and intentional way that no meaning is valid as another anymore, that none is preferred, thus no meaning can be expressed further. Stronger "défiles signifiantes" cannot exist at all, but one is important in the case of a procedure like Analytical Psychocatharsis, as can best be seen in the case of the dream and its interpretation. There, many meanings of a word and image nature circle around, but a meaning does not come about; only when matching, questioning and enriching with ideas about the dream does a massive narrowing of the increasingly significant dream material occur, which makes the true interpretation possible.

The concept of signifiers comes from linguistics, and in Lacanian psychoanalysis the signifiers are 'image-word-actings', that is, units composed of the imaginary (pictorial) and the symbolic (word-like), which permeate everything. They remind a little bit of what the astrophysicists today call the 'strings', wafer-thin vibrating strings, in short all that what already drove Goethe's Faust to want to know unconditionally "what holds the world together in its innermost". The world, the universe is the sum of signifiers, Lacan summarized. They are what - like the 'strings' in physics - hold the world together in its innermost. On the one hand it is about the 'crystalline, pictorial, imaginary and on the other hand about the 'linguistic', meaningful, symbolic signifiers, which cause everything. This dichotomy will run through my whole text, also to make understandable how one can outwit death.

It is, in fact, above all the imaginary side of *Analytic Psychocatharsis* which, closely (concretistically) connected with the symbolic one, could make death forgotten through insights into the innumerable forms of life. The emphasis of such a narrowing, scarcity, close combination is not found in any other comparable procedure. The concretistic, entangled, tightly interlaced, is also considered in physics as a culmination, in order to give the gap between spirit and matter a possibility of connection. I refer here to the physicist K. Barad, who, following the complementarity theory of N. Bohr and W. Heisenberg, has described compact entanglements of matter units distant from each other, so-called quanta. For them 'entanglement' is the decisive principle in all areas of being.[9]

---

[9] Barad, K., Verschränkungen (Entanglements), Merve (2015)

One must be careful here, of course, not to get into eso-teric waters. Because with Barad's conceptions one is mentally already close to being able to create a 'limited being' with yoga, meditation or anybody technique, in which in the very last moment of death the rest only has to be stripped off like the skin of a snake in order to be able to lead another own life. The concept of the 'strings' is likewise not much differently constructed, and - one calls them once 'ultra subtle strings' - could be ideally the entanglement existences in which unconsciously psychic and ultra subtle material could connect.

I come back to these speculations again, because they are fascinating not only in the usual mental fantasizing, but also in the experiences, which one makes in the afore-mentioned meditation or body techniques, to which also the *Analytic Psychocatharsis* would have reference. My own experiences are not sufficient to say definitive things, but have often made me feel this fascination in a more concrete way. The 'image-word-acting' are then combined in such a limited way that - if I didn't have a sound science as a basis - one could give in to the fasci-nations and word phantasties. But also the common sense tells one already so, for what one should prepare so many troubles to look at innumerable inner picture worlds.

Briefly summarized: In psychoanalysis one assumes two

basic forces, -drives, which Lacan calls the enunciation or speaking drive (instinct) and the perception or looking drive (instinct). I also call them symbolic and imaginary signifier, word- and image-acting, because they are close to the real. The real is not the reality, the reality, but the effectively true. Everything derives from their combinations and blockings. Sisyphus is thus, in my opinion, a picture-word-acting figure who exemplifies these forces also for the present time, and this apparently beyond death.

Of course, there is an absolute end somewhere, even if there have been several other ends in between. So also Sisyphus lives today only as this highly dramatic figure, but Zeus, the father god, what about him? We still have a father god today, after all, even if he has given up his wild adventures of seduction with all those many women. He has become a strict moral preacher. This transformation has been blamed on the transition from matrilineal to patrilineal structures, while Freud explained this transition from pubescent to serious god with the concept of 'patricide'. The even more adolescent rivals for power and women had killed the father, Freud says, but then, plagued by massive guilt, elevated him to the status of universal god. Father-murder and mother-incest could thus be called the psychoanalytic method of 'entanglement'. While god-father Zeus allowed himself everything, today's father-god - as Lacan claims - only consorts with corpses (since people come to him only after death).

Well, it will not be so blatant. Everything turns and 'entangles' itself once again in the circle. Even the scientists ask themselves, does not lead in the mathematical geometry the infinite straight line again back to the origin? Is not the end already there before the beginning? Even if it is the 'phantasm of fusion' postulated by the psychoanalysts that leads one back to the beginning (to the 'primary object', to the early mother, to the paradise conception, etc.), death is nevertheless outwitted, as with Sisyphus, only if the fusion consists only in an 'ultra-reduction', in the necessary, quite compact, concretist constrictions of the signifiers (this meat-grinder through which everything is turned). Sisyphus sees quite clearly that the funeral, together with its rites, laments and funeral songs, overbuilds, whitewashes and ultra-reduces the phenomenon of 'death'. And this is also the case in the statements of the unconscious, the *pass-words*, which are narrowed down by the *formula-words*.

So also Sisyphus must have seen this already in this way, because he did not keep to the external rules of the game, which ruled the world at that time and which today the natural scientists, the materialists, but also the sociologists, theologians and a hundred other scientists impose on us. Lacan unmasked the 'university discourse', i.e. the linguistic form of expression of the university, as a mediator function of purely 'wanting to know more and more', as a kind of 'more-pleasure' in the field of knowledge, knowing, research and technology, without questioning the actually important truth of all this knowledge. Knowledge must serve the truth and not the other way round, in that something like culture, physics, society etc. is presupposed as true and subordinated to a now new, profound, scientistically acquired knowledge. The truth possesses an "immanent function of origin", which Sisyphus has used mythically-genially, and which we can use today accompanied, supported, supported by science, but not dominated by it.

Even the truth of his sexual adventures has been felt by him, and not least because of that he had to cheat death. To mention only two of his erotic adventures: he raped - mas o meno - Antikleia, the daughter of Autolykos and he also seduced Tyro, the daughter of Salmoneus, who was known throughout Greece for her beauty. The latter had seized the Thessalian throne, which was awarded to Sisyphus, and so Sisyphus feigned noble intentions of love, although he was only concerned with the fulfilment of the Delphic oracle, which had advised him: "Bear children with your niece Tyro; they will avenge you"! So simple and clear and above all effective were the social behaviors at that time.

So we have to imagine Sisyphus after all, if not necessarily as a completely happy man, but at least as a wildly truth-knowing and from that at least not dissatisfied and similar to a god. Contrary to the common opinion today that Sisyphus is a negative example of antiquity, he was a hero in ancient Greece. He was an important and rich king in the area of Corinth, was a great patron (he donated the Isthmian Games), and he was clever (he convicted Autolykos, the master of thieves, who had the gift of changing the color of cattle and their horns and so could never be caught by Sisyphus marking the hooves of his cattle). Doesn't he have to be seen quite differently today? Ranke-Graves also argues that Sisyphus, like Oedipus, sought to replace the matrilineal kinship structure with a patrilineal one, that they were thus heroic pioneers opposed and punished by the matrilineal priesthoods. This is also an interpretation close to the creation myths.

Either way, the one who was able to cheat death twice is a great role model for man, even if an almost villainous image has stuck to him. This is what Sisyphus probably offers me and I should continue. As for his play with death, it makes one think that Freud, too, was very close to this theme with his eros and death instinct. But Freud's death drive cannot be an active drive (Eros-life as well as death and destruction drives were Freud's basic drives). An active drive directed toward death, proved to be an impossibility. And destructiveness comes rather from the first modes of identification, where one shifts what one cannot identify with concerning the same object into negativity and destructiveness - and so the death drive is in the concept of psychoanalysis nevertheless a constant counterpart of the lust for life. Here, it is primarily assigned to speaking, to the drive to express oneself or to speak, in that linguistic communication always contains an indeterminacy, a mediating function that is never completely perfect.

So one always talks somewhat past each other, and that is deadly. The semanticist G. Gamm, in any case, is of the opinion that one cannot say anything at all with certainty, no matter what one is talking about.[10] Whether one puts forward sentences with emphasis, with authorial power, with literary particularity or scientific wisdom, always a remainder remains totally veiled and carries with it, so to speak, the 'death of understanding'. Psychoanalytically, this leads to the fact that not only in conscious speech, but also in the unconscious, something must be constantly repeated in order to make itself heard. Freud spoke of the unconscious "repetition compulsion", which he just brought very close to the death drive, and which would have to be elucidated and resolved, something that never fully succeeds in the usual psychoanalysis. If this is what Sisyphus was able to overcome with cunning, he was already an excellent psychoanalyst at that time.

Because I remind again of the signifiers, on whose level everything takes place, which has to do with the people and whose sum represents world and universe. Certainly there is a 'Higgs field', which one could prove physically in 2017 in the LHC in Geneva and which fixes all ele-

---

[10] Gamm, G., Nicht nichts, Studien zu einer Semantik des Unbestimmbaren (Not Nothing, Studies on semantics of the indeterminate), Suhrkamp (2000) p. 227.

mentary particles. And one can certainly also speak of God and the regularities of the society with the same definiteness and right, but one does not get away from the 'image-word-acting'. Rightly someone once claimed that if this 'image-word-acting' M o o n did not exist, the earth satellite would not give existence.

One would see occasionally something bright in the firmament, a spot in the visual total area, a luminescence among other luminescences, but M o o n? Moon what? Yes Moon, a real thing that is a breakaway from the Earth, a giant sphere orbiting the Earth illuminated by the Sun, its own central disk of light, a symbol that can now be definitely grasped because it has its own name. Without name no being. That had been, what Sisyphus could take advantage of the death, when he said to Persephone, where no funeral, no rite, no death prayer exists, there is also no death. And as long as I can still negotiate with you, there exists an intermediate realm, where one is already believed dead, but still can come back once more to the glorious life on earth. Didn't Orpheus, in order to get his Eurydice out of Hades, also get so far into the realm of the dead that he was able to soothe Cerberus, the hound of hell, with his wonderful music that he forgot to bark and Tartarus then also allowed Orpheus to take his wife with him.

In any case, many neighbors today would be happy if they could teach the dogs to forget to bark by using sounds and flattering words. How to Do Things with

Words', that one can create realities with words, sounds, even applies to mathematics, where one believed to need only numbers and a few arithmetic signs like + or -.[11] In reality, one has to set up axioms or even algorithms, calculation rules formulated linguistically. Now I think that just when one excludes thoughts and emotions and everything else like in a meditation, something significant appears nevertheless and announces itself like for example: "What offers Sisyphus"? Apart from the mythical story, which is about his greatness, but also about his shameful deeds, I also remembered a few things from earlier years, which I would probably still have to work through: didn't I also once try to outsmart death with sex, because this is also how one has to understand Sisyphus' love adventures?

Yes of course, that is probably the sense of sex at all. Doesn't the punishment of Sisyphus - if one interprets it in a figurative sense - consist exactly in dragging the constant erotic desire, the sex and love addiction, the 'object of desire' up to the heights, where it, however, always falls down again, gets lost and yet doesn't disappear, because the satisfaction only lasts for a short time? Yes and no. Sisyphus loves his rock, his stone, because "there is no fate that cannot be overcome by contempt (mépris)", Camus writes. Mépris also means contempt, because Sisyphus does not attach a high value to the

---

[11] Austin, J. L., How to Do Things with Words, Urmson (2018)

whole thing; for him, overcoming death is the most important thing.

Lacan emphasized on every third page of his books that sex does not exist, because nothing of it could be logically said, written down, defined. The sexual relationship would always fail, constantly miss, never sustainably satisfy, because the man would always ejaculate at the climax (on Sisyphus' hill) of his anxiety, knowing no more. Lacan therefore called the erotic relationship a "Freudian failure", a fluff, a failure to succeed, an illusory relationship, because at the climax the man becomes a helpless child who often also slurs a quite foolish phrase. And the woman knows that now it was again nothing with the intimate togetherness. But even with his greed for money and fame, the man usually doesn't know what to do at the peak of his success. This also shows Sisyphus as a human ruler.

Freud's effort was about nothing else than to show the overvaluation of sex as a "humiliator in love life". In a dream of his famous patient Dora, the parental home is on fire, the mother wants to quickly save her jewelry box, whereupon the father says something like: should we burn because of your stupid box? The box symbolizes the female organ, and it is the man who is afraid of losing it. And that's exactly why Dora had to be a lesbian, because she also said to herself: should I have to get married to a man because of this stupid thing? Sex can make you deathly unhappy, because like sex, death gives no answer.

If a two-hundred-fold billionaire like Warren Buffet loses only one billion, he is deadly unhappy, and that is because it is called b i l l i o n and not one dollar out of two hundred, but the relation is the same. It behaves like with the moon, in that comparatively the word billion determines the horror of the loss, not the real relation of the money. Not the number, but the number word does its part. The billionaire does not love his money at all, it only excites him, it is his fetish, and he takes it too seriously. He is perverse. The purpose of life, the heroic goal as such, is actually not decisively affected by it. Sisyphus, on the other hand, loves his stone, but he also respects it. In any case, it is the symbol of the attempt to win and to overcome desire. But back to the main theme, to outsmarting death.

3. Life while Dying

Cheating, outsmarting death two times is not meant to be a baseless statement. I take the sentence quite seriously, even if I do not take it in the way an ultraorthodox Christian or Muslim does, who repeatedly dreams of a very specific life after the life he is currently living. To understand what the afterlife is, Lacan believes, one must die, or rather have experienced, two deaths in this world. For one does not experience the last death, even Sisyphus did not witness the very last end. He only died two deaths before, and that was meant completely in Lacan's psychoanalytical sense. Lacan took over the idea of two deaths from the infamous Marquis de Sade, who claimed that a normal death is not enough for a perfect murder, one must then also completely cut up and crush the dead. Otherwise life would arise again from the same building components, which still remained with this first dying and with it a total reorganization would not be possible. Because this is necessary if one looks at the catastrophic world of that time as of today.

Now the opinion of the good Marquis is little relevant, because if the last word, which the murdered and crushed could still breathe before itself, was heard, it could survive eternally and at least still so much announce from the building blocks that there would be no more question of the total extinction. De Sade did not know that rumors could be immortal, as the philosopher of religion R. Spaemann claimed of God. His thesis that God is an "immortal rumor" was not meant negatively. On the contrary, nothing is more alive and more lively than what is whispered and whispered behind closed doors. And if the rumor is immortal on top of that, it fits God much better than the devotional images of an old, bearded man whose sayings everyone knows by heart. De Sade's second death is only a delusion of annihilation, which served Lacan only as a model for the first death, i.e. for the one that should be clearly definable and transparent, in order to be able to distinguish exactly between this world and the hereafter. This first death, then, has to do with the regressive, with that which leads back to psychic beginnings.

The stories about the two deaths also remind immediately of the discussion which is led at present once again about the so-called organ donation. The removal of organs, known as the 'objection solution', which can be carried out on anyone who has died suddenly or on accident victims if there is no objection to the removal, is rejected by very many people because they say that the final time of death cannot be clearly determined. Even modern neurological techniques for determining brain death would not be sufficient. Even functional nuclear spin tomographies would not change anything in this respect, and if one investigates it very precisely, the critics are not wrong. One should only let the dead rest for a considerable time until one can speak of a real end, that is, until he has reached his real second or multiple and finally very last death.

As a physician, I have seen many people die, and in the case of some who remained lying at home for a long time, I could share the relatives' view that, for example, the facial expression of the deceased had still changed slightly after some time. It impressed in a completely different way , than at the early time, at which one would have had to carry out an organ removal at the latest. Often the facial expression was more relaxed or seemed more reassuring than at the moment which one would have had to regard as his outwardly perceived dying in order to still come in time to the transplantative intervention. There is probably something to it, that the 'soul' 'leaves' the body in a somewhat later moment, as religious ideas suggest.

Only the word 'leaving' is not chosen quite right, because I believe that the 'soul' still remains in the brain metabolism, if one can grasp this as being in a minimal molecular state or even in a still underlying, perhaps quite unconscious level, where subtle processes still go much further than we can definitely state today. The deceased who is lying in this way and who is not yet medically identified by the classical signs such as lividity and rigor mortis, and who is declared in the death certificate, may really need some more time for himself before we really release him for burial. Yes, even after death determined by the most modern technology (EEg, angiography, etc.)

some kind of life seems to continue for a while. However, in many types of organ removal, this time is significantly shortened.

Just recently (Holy Week 2019), neuroscientist Nedan Sestan published an article in the prestigious journal Nature, wherein he described how brain cells in animals still gave neurological signs of life hours after their death and thus without oxygen. "The researchers took tissue samples of the brain and were able to show that its neurons exchanged electrical signals after appropriate stimulation. The death of brain cells after oxygen deprivation was apparently a gradual and longer lasting process". [12] So there is not only a brain metabolism as I mentioned above, but there is an information exchange in the neuronal network of the brain.[13] But this can also have reference to the network of the unconscious, which is after all a network of word-image-acting or one of components of topology.[14]

Topology has many concrete relations to neuronal networks and to the unconscious psychical. Lacan explained many psychic-unconscious structures with topo-

---

[12] Albrecht, J., Brendler, M., Report of FAS (Frankfurt Gen. Journal) from 21. 4. 2019. S. 53

[13] People have always talked about stages of death, but scientific proof is worth more than myth.

[14] Hummel, von, G., Phoneme & Pixel, BoD (2019), where I refer to Einsteinian geometry, showing structures as they probably exist between the unconscious and the brain.

logical figures, since these image-word-actors represent mental aspects such as aspiration and desire as the two sides of a single surface (see figure above, where different topologies are shown). And indeed, the German Nobel Prize winner K. von Klitzing himself has been able to prove such structures in physical solid bodies (so-called quantum Hall effect), which again reminds of Barad's entanglement realities, which are well combined in such topological structures, no matter how and what has been found and said about it in the different sciences. All this serves only a general illustrative purpose for the understanding of energetic, net-like distributions..

Klein-Bottle   Möbiusband   Hopf-Fibration

For much more important is what has been further stated in the discussion of this neuroscientific study by N. Sestan in Nature. For one thing, that these neuron signals could be detected up to six hours after the death of the animal and thus without oxygen supply.[15] On the other

---

[15] I assume that with the human being it is not about such a long time. Above all, if one wants to consider the valuable part existing in it, it is perhaps only about several minutes. But in this case one reckons with the fixed time calculation of

hand it was argued that in this time after death, despite the continuing reaction signs with no kind of reanimation, real life, i.e. brain activity with "higher functions" could be expected again. What should be the purpose of continuing to explore such an inferior life? Life would thus be terminated one way or another and thus the study would not be very interesting, the author claims. But what does really terminated mean here and what, moreover, does "higher brain functions" mean?

As mentioned by the terms regression, mental return, involution to early childhood stages of experience, such states are known in psychology and neurology as necessary and much more important for certain recovery and restoration processes than the fully conscious mental state. One does not speak then of 'deeper brain functions', but of more elementary, more primal or - as Freud did - of the " primordial repressed ", i.e. a state of a very first repression or psychoanalytic necessity, with which then the less repressed areas can be explained. Just these more elementary states are significant and important for life in the original sense, in the unconscious and neurologically more central brain regions. Especially the neurologist A. R. Lurija established a connection of brain and unconscious decades ago, relating the Freudian 'Id', i.e. the reservoir of driving forces with midbrain and diencephalic regions. So it is not about the cerebrum and

---

the everyday-conscious psyche and not with that which becomes experienceable in this intermediate realm.

its so-called "higher brain functions", which are essential for the basis of the soul, but about the more elementary functions.

The ego, ego-ideal and superego, the planning and all-thinking frontal brain, as well as the isolated word and image processing (in the temporal and in the posterior lobe) only disturb the basic soul, which comes into play in dreams, but also in meditation, in certain religious experiences, in psychoanalysis and especially in the dying process. But this aspect is especially important when it comes to life in death, which I would prefer to call life in death (as opposed to life after death). For a possible reanimation and return to so-called "higher brain functions" (with which, moreover, often the most terrible things are done), this kind of life naturally no longer plays a role. But that is also not necessary. Perhaps it is even one of the most important phases in the purely elementary psychical.

But all the more important is this still for hours lasting phase of neuro-psychic processes, as Sestan researched it. In the vernacular it has always been said that in the last moments of leaving, drifting away, the whole life runs before you again like in a movie. But I don't believe that it is like that and it doesn't bring anything, because it doesn't convey a solution. This is also the reason why I have spoken about the steps with which one can learn to die even before the very last death, which is, already having had similar experiences with regression, mental withdrawal and processing of primary psychic structures.

Between the life with "higher brain functions" and the final death there is obviously a perhaps quite extended intermediate realm. So one could also say that life has to be outwitted, even in death (or at least in dying) to last a little bit longer. For what we need is a subject 'without a head', as Lacan says, that is, without headiness as repre-sented by the "higher brain performances".[16] Too much thinking, calculating, feeling up and down or even brooding is only a handicap. The unconscious know-ledge of truth pushes outward, but directly (from the irrational to the rational) - as emphasized above - the unconscious can no longer accomplish such an aware-ness in the dying state. But for this the soul finds in this state the perfect limitation of inside and outside, i.e. it doesn't take this difference for important anymore and still creates the most essential combinations of these two basic elements.

It needs this instrument of the combination of the word-image-acting, this purely formal "key-sentence" ma-chine, in order to create the spark of the real meaning, whereby the point of meaning, the actual metaphor, is especially achieved by the fact that "the greatest dispari-ty of the designated images is required". That is, in order to achieve full effect in the unconscious, the

---

[16] Lacan, J., Seminaire XI, Seuil (1964) S. 165

O.R.S.A.C.E.R.A.M. mentioned above as an example must not coalesce into a superficial sense, rather, through the great disparity of the meanings it contains, it must be provoked that the unconscious itself can give out its own, its own sense (thus, after all, the analyst interprets out of the nonsense of the dream the true sense of the dreamer).

The ego, ego-ideal and superego, the planning and all-thinking frontal brain, as well as the isolated word and image processing (in the temporal and in the posterior lobe) only disturb the basic soul, which comes into play in dreams, but also in meditation, in certain religious experiences, in psychoanalysis and especially in the dying process. But this aspect is especially important when it comes to life w h i l e dying, which I would prefer even to call life in the m i d d l e of death (as opposed to life after death). For a possible reanimation and return to so-called "higher brain functions" (with which, moreover, often the most terrible things are done), this kind of life naturally no longer plays a role.

But all the more important is this still for hours lasting phase of neuro-psychic processes, as Sestan researched it. In the vernacular it has always been said that in the last moments of leaving, drifting away, the whole life runs before you again like in a movie. But I don't believe that it is like that and it doesn't bring anything, because it doesn't convey a solution. This is also the reason why I have spoken about the steps with which one can learn to die even before the very last death, which is, already having had similar experiences with regression, mental withdrawal and processing of primary psychic structures.

Between the life with "higher brain functions" and the final death there is obviously a perhaps quite extended intermediate realm. So one could also say that life has to be outsmarted, even in death (or at least in dying) to last a little bit longer. For what we need is a subject 'without a head', as Lacan says, that is, without headiness as represented by the "higher brain performances".[17] The unconscious knowledge of truth pushes outward, but directly (from the irrational to the rational) – as emphasized above – the unconscious can no longer accomplish such an awareness in the dying state. But for this the soul finds in this state the perfect limitation of inside and outside, i.e. it doesn't take this difference for important anymore and still creates the most essential combinations of these two basic elements, the image- und word-acting.

It needs this instrument of the combination of the word-image-acting, this purely formal 'key-sentence' machine, in order to create the spark of the real meaning, whereby the point of meaning, the actual metaphor, is especially achieved by the fact that "the greatest disparity of the designated images is required". That is, in order to achieve full effect in the unconscious, the O.R.S.A.C.E.

---

[17] Lacan, J., Seminaire XI, Seuil (1964) S. 165

R.A.M. mentioned above as an example must not coalesce into a superficial sense, rather, through the great
disparity of the meanings it contains, it must be provoked that the unconscious itself can give out its own, its
own sense (thus, after all, the analyst interprets out of the
nonsense of the dream the true sense of the dreamer).[18]

But such a process is also produced in dying, where the
soul must not be disturbed by the conscious, and everything with it depends on how far it has already found
itself in a suitable, successful, optimal word-picture
combination in the life before. From the life in the middle of death, from the life while dying has therefore he
predominantly something, who is already prepared for it,
which does not exclude that the majority of the people,
who have brought the usual life to a good maturity, profit just the same from it. However, the procedure of *Analytic Psychocatharsis* can still be a help, because the
concept of maturity can be defined even more broadly by
it.

The philosopher A. Schopenhauer also presents the pure
subject, i.e. the subject 'without head', as immortal:
"True, space is only in my head; but empirically my head
is in space". The head is thus levelled off in favor of the
"conception, which is the primordial, which breaks down
into object and subject. The subject is that which cogniz-

---

[18] Freud spoke of "key sentences" in dreams, for which one
no longer needs an interpretation at all, but which one can
read off the page like the *pass-words*.

es everything and is cognized by none. It is the 'carrier of the world', the condition of all appearing, of all object. The empirical subject is only appearance, conditioned by the organism. The 'pure subject of cognition', on the other hand, never becomes object, is timeless, supra-individual, will-less, unknowable, correlate of the 'idea', not subject to the theorem of the reason, eternal. The subject recognizes itself only as a willing, not, as a cognizing".[19]

In other words, this world stops in the body (brain) only very slowly where the hereafter begins just as well slowly, so that the striving person is familiar with both states of a completely subject-related kind when he has learned to die well. Because he must have learned this already a little bit, the time at the end is not sufficient otherwise much, in order to be able to die 'experienced', matured, clarified and with reduced brain functions. So with the two deaths in this world is meant something that perhaps everyone experiences anyway in his life not only once, when he got into great crises, illnesses, depressions, despair, physical injuries and many other seriously impairing things and has already learned what dying is probably about.

Especially in such a procedure as psychoanalysis, one is put into a regressive state, into a return to earliest childlike experiences and their meanings, so that one can

---

[19] Schopenhauer, A., On the fourfold root of the theorem of the sufficient reason, Hofenberg (2016).

speak here of dying in the middle of life, in the middle of the therapist's consulting room. This is even more true for the method of *Analytic Psychocatharsis*, which I inaugurated, and which one practices largely alone at home, and in which one gets into an almost simultaneous regressive-progressive state. This state thus leads back and nevertheless in the same moment also includes a progressive experience - thanks to the precise, compact *formula-words* - which further leads into the experience of the identity-, or *pass-words*.

This realm between life and death also plays a major role in the legend of Orpheus and Eurydice. In this myth, intense love is at the center, even though the two loving protagonists, Orpheus and Eurydice, were then unable to remain bound in love any longer. As is known, Orpheus used his 'higher brain functions' (his musical knowledge) in an equally fatal way, namely the reassurance, the logical retrospect, that his wife would really follow him into life, and thus - as said before - the whole thing does not work, not anymore. The saga, however, takes place exactly in such an intermediate realm, where the living could enter and the dead could come out again - in modern terms - an alternation of psychic regression and progression.

Was perhaps the love not strong enough? The Tibetan Book of the Dead is also about this intermediate realm, but here about the time between death and rebirth.[20] And it is about the love for certain gods and not about one among humans. Obviously, the Tibetan monks assumed that the dying person in this initial phase is still accessible to loudly recited chants and songs. Other mystics have also often used such formulations as that of 'dying in life', the apostle Paul even said that he "dies daily in Christ".

Now daily is probably too much, his regression-progression probably did not last long, so it had to be repeated daily. I must admit that for *Analytic Psychocatharsis* daily exercises are also quite good - even if not necessary. There are also always seminars, books and courses offered on the subject of 'learning to die'. The best known and initially also the most well-founded on the subject of dying were and still are the remarks of the professor of medicine and psychiatrist E. Kübler-Ross from the end of the last century and the beginning of this century. She spoke with numerous dying people, researched the different phases of dying and published scientific works about it.[21]

Still in the mid-seventies, however, the professional psychiatrist turned into a New Age healer. She said that death does not exist and twice founded 'spiritual centers' where she taught the meeting and overcoming of death

---

[20] Hauf, M., Das Tibetanische Totenbuch (The Tibetian Book of Death), Piper (2003)

[21] Kübler-Ross, E., On Death and Dying, SCRIBNER (2014)

with ideas going as far as spiritualism and completely spiritual abstractions. However, both centers were completely destroyed by fires soon after their opening, as if, in the sense of a bad omen, the other world had raged against her new teachings to show what awaits one there. After a stroke and increasing serious illnesses, Kübler-Ross became aggressive against herself and the world and wailed in despair about her approaching end. Her sisters accused her of not being able to let go, even though she had told everyone about life after death, and wrote to her at the end, "Beth, stop that spinning stuff. Keep your feet on the ground. Tell what you know, but no more".[22]

Kübler-Ross was not so completely wrong, however, because if one soars far up with a great deal of love for oneself and for everything and for everyone else, it may already be possible that one no longer notices death intellectually because of all the spiritualization. And then it is possibly also possible that the soul remains in the brain - as described above - for a longer time than usual with a lot of refinement exercises. But then one should speak more fairly of a life while dying and not of a life after death as Kübler-Ross did. Because why should the life after death not have a death again, after which then another life after death takes place . . . etc. Life in dying is certainly very fulfilling, only you have to know a little bit about it, and that also has something to do with love.

---

[22] Quotation from Wikipedia about Elisabeth Kübler-Ross

Only it is rather a love to oneself, regarding which the psychoanalyst M. Mitscherlich titled her last book: "A love to oneself that makes happy".[23] This sounds a bit narcissistic, but she did not mean it that way. It had to do with the love for her work, that is, with what is called the 'detached love" the detached, the made-up removal, the somewhat detached love that also makes the psychoanalyst.[24] For in order that the psychoanalyst does not fall prey to a completely absorbing identification with his patient, he needs a certain distance, a minimal separateness. Empathy is good, but total empathy helps no one, and so love in psychoanalysis must be detached from ties, separated from too much closeness, and protected from intimacy. But Mitscherlich would have written much better: "A love for oneself as the Other ..". or "A love for one's own unconscious as that which is still unfinished, as that which is very differently geared in oneself".

Not only to the external other, also to oneself this love is characterized by a slight, discrete distance, which is suitable for regressing, for 'dying in life', where one meets the other in oneself, the truth-mirror of the soul. It is not

---

[23] Mitscherlich, M., Eine Liebe zu sich selbst, die glücklich macht, S. Fischer (2013)

[24] Kohon, G., Love in a time of madness. In Green & Kohon: Love and its vicissitudes, Routledge (2005) S. 41 – 100. The author speaks from the 'detached love'. I would rather say ‚disengaged love'.

good to be immoderately in love with oneself until the end, narcissistic or otherwise, just as it is not helpful to come to an end prematurely in the middle of love entanglements with other people. This is the only way to understand Lacan's phrase that "there is always some delight of death in love, a death, however, that we cannot impose on ourselves".[25] This is to say that one does not overcome death with a suicide, and one certainly cannot outwit it and have the delights that come with it. In Yasushi Inoue's novel, too, it was suggested that 'love loosened and a little made up' is more complete than one exalted to the high altar.

One could support all this also with the modern chaos theory. For F. Cramer, a co-founder of the chaos theory, Eros and love is a profound resonance, the principle of life and love that takes place in recurring, cyclic times, which Cramer contrasts with an irreversible, chaotically collapsing and thus non-resonant time.[26] Cramer thus tries to understand love and Eros as "harmonious mood and consonance", but also to represent it as something unspeakable, chaotic, which cannot be thought in terms of time and order. All the forms of usual love are thus contrasted with 'chaos/love', which has no resonance and yet is strong, pervasive.

---

[25] Lacan, J., Die Übertragung (The Transference), Seminar VIII, Report from 15. 5. 61
[26] Cramer, F., Symphonie des Lebendigen (Symphony of the Living), Insel (1998).

Thus Cramer rightly stands against the value of resonance propagated in a very extensive work by the sociologist H. Rosa.[27] For Rosa meticulously attempts to prove that everywhere, in all relationships and constitutions, resonance is ultimately to be found, and that it is essential for universal understanding. "If acceleration is the problem, then resonance may be the solution. This, in the shortest possible formula, is the core thesis of Rosa's book", reads the blurb. The reviewer of the SZ, J. Bisky, for all his sympathy for the longing for a successful world, lacks an appreciation of the actual ones, and so the more than 815 pages of Rosa's book are agonizing.

The delights, the bliss, of death can, of course, also have something to do with the 'longing for fusion', for merger, which I already described at the beginning as a form of a basic phantasm, and which represents a desire for death mixed with love.[28] One wants to repeat something that has not yet come to pass in life, has not been said, has not been admitted and revealed or has been lost forever. Like the black holes in physics, the 'merging phantasm' has incredible attraction, although it is empty, is primordial lack, gap, nothingness. We do not recover from the separation that became reality at birth, namely not only

[27] Rosa, H., Resonanz, eine Soziologie der Weltbeziehung (Resonance. A Sociology of the World Relationship), Suhrkamp (2019).

[28] Lacan, J., Seminar VIII, Passagen-Verlag (2008) S. 234

the separation from the mother, but also from half of the child's body (placenta, which belongs to the child and not to the mother). We do not recover from this separation and cling to the objects of life? But if we can go beyond separation and loss, we can enjoy the delights.[29]

For the delights do not require the "higher brain powers". It seems to be so that "higher brain performances" come to great bloom only with a few quite detached philosophers like I. Kant, Schopenhauer or modern authors who rave about the 'cultural memory' of mankind. Yet Freud had already made it clear that there is a 'malaise in culture' (in and not of culture), and that the real memory is the unconscious, which opens up when we die, whereas otherwise in ordinary life it remembers everything only badly, but at the same time has stored it firmly. The elaborate work of repression prevents memory, but thoroughly imprisons it. That's why it's good to have already worked through a few things as a precaution for these last six hours in the intermediate realm of death.

Regardless of whether you understand it this way or not, I will describe the process that is ultimately at issue here once again using the phenomenon of so-called 'near-death experiences'. I have already spoken of the regressive state, of a return to the most original soul. To this - as one could also say: 'neuropsychological regressing' -

---

[29] That deals with the experience in *Analytic Psychocatharsis.*

the reports of frequently described near-death experiences fit quite well. People tell that they had the feeling as if they had stepped out of their body and could see themselves from above. When one steps out of oneself, i.e. centers

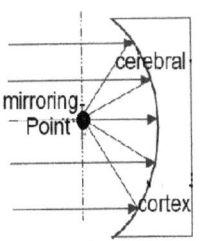

oneself in one's head in the mirror or subject point of the nervous system and at the same time loses oneself completely, let's go totally or goes into a trance, one enters exactly into the focal point which is given by the hemisphere sitting on the base of the skull, which after all acts like a concave mirror. The concave, reflective nerve cell layer that spot-reflects 'rays' (nerve currents) coming from the body and other brain layers in the center of the hemisphere (see illustration above) produces experiences of apparent clairvoyance and hallucinations, but also of what Lacan calls the 'ultrasubjective radiance' that I simplistically call the Id *Rays* in many other publications.

Lacan clearly elaborated this point in his 'Mirror Stage as the Builder of the Ego Function'. One sees oneself as a whole only virtually in the Other and if one can 'see' out of the 'light' point, the flash point, point of the brain mirror, then because one is so reduced and regressed in this *Rays* of the focal point, so that one perceives oneself as if clairvoyantly.[30] One only swims in the pixels, one is

---

[30] The Other to be written in capital letters, which plays an important role in Lacan, I have already described earlier as

only image-reality, unconscious seeing. This is exactly what people experience in so-called near-death experiences. It is about the same multiple perception that film theorists often report.

One is in the cinema completely in the attention of the

Other (in the attention of the total film, of the converging spectator-, camera-, actor- and director-gaze). And so one 'sees' oneself - multiply-fanned - as from the point of view of the Other. But in the reality of the cinema or the near-death-experience one changes in this moment only from this bundled Id *Rays* and its sharpened imaginary order into the Id *Speaks* of the symbolic world. Also this Id *Speaks* is the linguistic, symbolic counterpart to the Id *Rays* of the most primary unconscious processes, as they were conceived by Freud and Lacan on the basis of looking and speaking instinct (or drive) and I conceive them here as a combination of the word-image-acting.

For it is as if in this moment of multiple perception, in the moment of Id *Rays*, there is also a very rudimentary speaking, an Id *Speaks,* which says as in a command tone: "Look at you", " "Watch", which thus gives an exclamation of highest fear or also only most glaring astonishment, and so one sees oneself just in the near-death experience as if from above or in the film as if

---

truth-mirror. It is the virtual body of the Id *Rays* in its connection to the Id *Speaks*, to which I want to give further explanations immediately.

perceived from a completely different perspective.[31] The unconscious connected with the brain knows itself lying there in the near-death experience and translates the "look" into the hallucination of really looking at oneself. The near-death experience is the vocal imperative of an all-seeing. It is unconsciously 'seen' and 'spoken'.

But the imperative - isn't it exactly a beginning of the command, the password, of speaking at all? The linguists say that the first words of man were not designations for objects, but password words, identity words, on the basis of which one could confirm and recognize each other. Security and trust were in the first place required and not words with which one could distinguish water from wood by calling them so. Only later did other words make themselves possible, words that could be spoken with special emphasis, reinforced by repetition, to become the final language. Lacan strictly meant that the pre-human knew only a signal language and no symbol language. As in the chirping of birds, he could give sound signals, but except for the trilling of love desire and territorial claims, no statement was possible for him.

---

[31] So here it is about a " look for the first time", (a premiére vu in contrast to a deja vu), which on the other hand is followed by a "always already as primary linguistically said" (a deja raconte). This again reminds us of the film, where even 'special effects' seem to us quite natural or of the dream, where it seems quite natural that 'science fiction' scenes take place, which we take for completely real.

Only when he could repeat a sound sequence emphasized and consciously, when he could give an emotion, an astonishment, an affect with the same sound sequence once again and then again and again with special emphasis, the symbol, the first word was born and man was man. In the birdsong the sound sequences are not always consistently the same, and even if they are, they are not presented with a kind of surprise, increasingly serious emphasis and consciousness. The pure phonetic imagery has become a wordiness and signification that could be perpetuated with increasing understanding. Exactly this beginning of speaking, the Id *Speaks*, the phonematic, is equally activated in the near-death experience as well as the narrowly reduced seeing of the Id *Rays* of the pure pixel world.

In general, I find it significant that when it comes to such an elementary and impressive experience as that of near-death, the Id *Rays / Speaks* are completely moved together, interconnected. It deals with the mirror-gaze of an echo-discourse, about the ultimate combinatorics of desire and death.[32] Why do we actually speak of near-death, since it is the deepest possible state of meditation and the real death is still far away? The whole thing resembles again a life in dying, the death in this world, which must follow then still another for the comprehension of the hereafter. Only, of course, one cannot prac-

---

[32] This also applies to the movie, if it is really good, i.e. gripping, elementary true and effective.

tice near-death experiences beforehand to learn this 'dying' of which so many clever sentences have been written without real practical and scientifically based instructions. The term near-death is a falsifying designation for a trauma-conditioned hallucination.

But briefly a reference to the play of the Brandner Kasper from the year 1871, which is very popular with the population of Bavaria and which is also about life in the confrontation with death. Brandner Kasper also manages to outsmart death (almost) twice. The first time he gets Death drunk and tricks him into playing cards. Death promises him another eighteen years of life, but is severely reprimanded for this in heaven by the archangel Michael, who plays the same role here as Zeus does with Sisyphus. So Death tries again soon after to bring the Brandner Kasper home. After much back and forth, they both agree on a deal: Brandner Kaspar is allowed to look into paradise for a while, where he can see his deceased relatives in wonderful landscapes, which finally convinces him to follow Death.

Well, the thing already sounds very Catholic; the purgatory that catches up with Sisyphus is clearly left out in this play - at the expense of the principle of reality - because actually the Brandner Kasper has committed a few crimes on the basis of which one normally does not get into paradise.[33] The underlying conclusion is that the

---

[33] In Freud, there is a pleasure principle and a reality principle that balance each other out.

Bavarians are to be kept happy and always believe that their godly government has everything under control. This is still true today after more than a hundred years. But the decisive question, how to outwit death in a modern and "logically practical" form, has not yet been properly addressed, let alone answered.[34] Because the very last death is not to be avoided, it is to be used only for a valuable experience.

Incidentally, death is not the inorganic, as Freud still thought and what he considered the goal of life. The inorganic is only the hardened, totally rigid, motionless. That is why the uncanny has nothing to do with death, but is only the fear of it. Also, we always have half inorganic, apparently dead in the form of the skellet in us, and are just as the computer animations of artificial intelligence on chips, which will be implanted in us in the future, not new. Drugs, the constant TV bombardment, bad habits and the hundred rituals of everyday life and much more mean a constant rigidity, stiffness, immobility in and around us. With that, you don't learn to die, you just remain lifeless.

The death itself namely, the last one hundred percent comes about through the end of the enjoyment of life. No more enjoyment of life can mean to die long before the physical decay: in mental confusion, dementia, addiction and ideological delusion. Therefore it is advanta-

---

[34] Lacan also called psychoanalysis a 'logical practice'.

geous to be already on a first-name basis with death in scientifically founded meditation, to speak with it like Luther did it (he spoke with the devil, who is nothing else than a twin of death). And so also the artificial intelligence will be the death only if one cannot switch it off in time. The same applies to the body, with which one dies only if one has not united the body images in time to a single ray point, mirror point, in the *Rays* in the *Speaks*.

Because it is probably possible by an intensive meditative, psychoanalytical, a somehow renewed self-sublimating training or something else similar to fake, imitate or reproduce a dying in life, which is to construct as authentic as possible, in order to profit from it for the actual life. In the next chapter, I will try to show how this has perhaps already been achieved or at least how far it has gone and how it has been attempted. And how it can be revived today in a scientifically secured way. Because only in this way it makes sense to answer anew the question about life w h i l e dying, as it was taken up, among other things, by the article in the journal Nature.

4. Attempts at Resuscitation

In order to 'die' and to be 'reborn', it is best not to go to the South Seas or to all the tourist areas overflowing with the desire for the fascinating and the strange, only to encounter the same and the familiar again. No, you go to the northeast of Asia, to the deserted plains and hilly landscapes of the Amur, Asia's Amazon, to let yourself be carried away by its lazily flowing waters. Amur, that already sounds like the French l`amour, Chinese 'Hei-long' Jiang, Black Dragon, because the river crosses the northernmost China and is really also 'healing' (German 'Heilung') for the soul. Tundra, taiga forests, pines, steppes and grasslands and the hum of an ancient melody from the prehistory of man . . . .

And yet, despite all this, despite the distance, the monk-ish solitude and the beguiling name, the Amur region does not let you completely outsmart death. But even so-called reincarnation theories don't really let you resur-rect. Instead of being in the unconscious, these people relate 'déjà vu', the having seen, having experienced, having been there before, to a real past life. They do not realize that this experience goes unnoticed with the in-sistence of a 'jamais-raconté' (never told before) in the unconscious (the inverse version from footnote 28). Be-cause something has never been said, never been proper-ly told, never been properly admitted and effectively revealed (against typical psychoanalytic resistances), even though it urges it in the unconscious, certain scenes can appear so psychically over-occupied that they seem - similar to near-death experiences - as if they have already been experienced and seen. It is reminiscent of the work of the philosopher Merleau-Ponty, in which the "invisible" is ultimately a speaking, which becomes clear at the latest when one assigns to perception the things as visible and to language the invisible meanings.[35]

One can see in Merleau-Ponty that he is very close to the essential with his formulas, there, for example, where he speaks of the "flesh", of the libidinous (the Freudian libido, the Eros energy) , which smolders along like an eternally unredeemed desire in its "redness": the "flesh as visibility and as the place of an inscription of truth", he writes regarding these opposites of the image- and the word-acting. He does not speak of the red, also not of the redness, but of the essence of the flesh and of the desire, of the "R(aw)dness" (German: "Ro(h)(t)heit") - yes, one must say it in such a way, because so everything is in it, what also the painter Rupert Geiger, who painted almost only pictures in red, claimed: Red tones lying very close to each other (like Red and Raw) arouse a special impression, an examination of this color, which, seen in this way, gives much more than a red, which is placed next to a blue or yellow.

---

[35] Merleau-Ponty, M., Das Sichtbare und das Unsichtbare (The Visible and the Invisible), W. Fink Verlag (1994) S. 273

As in the experience of the Amur, where one is strength-
ened by the inertia and the melodiousness of the river in
this completely deserted landscape, one comes back
reincarnatively, that is, around two corners, to one's own
past, but one does not learn what really counts, what
makes the mathematics of life come together as directly
as possible. One is convinced to go into the film of one's
own past, some of it seems believable, some of it, in
turn, doesn't quite fit with today. "Even before the actual
human relations come into being, certain relations are
already determined", Lacan proclaimed in his eleventh
seminar, and this could fit well with the monotonous and
yet so murmuring, speaking river landscape. "For nature
provides signifiers.[36] Even before all experience, before
all individual deduction, and before any collective experience at all . . . settle down, there is something that or-
ganizes this field and inscribes the first lines of force in
it . . . the function of an initial classification".

And further: "What is important for us is that we recognize here the level on which - even before any formation
of a subject that thinks - it already counts, on which it is
counted. What is important is that in this being counted,
a counting is already there".[37] A counting becomes very

---

[36] Even first decisive images like sun, moon and stars can -
according to Lacan - have meaning in the sense of primary
language symbols as imaginary signifiers.

[37] Lacan, J., Die vier Grundbegriffe der Psychoanalyse (The
four Basic Terms of Psychoanalysis, Walter (1980) S. 26

quickly a human counting, is also soon a telling, an Id *Speaks*, as I have tried to imitate by murmuring the Amur. This "universal murmuring", as Lacan also calls the unconscious, as if it were already trying to make this counting quite clear and understandable, must probably be left in a certain blur for the time being. But this much can already be said, this saying, this Id *Speaks*, is opposed by the field of the first lines of power, which thus can be called shortened an Id *Rays*, because rays or an 'appearance' still more vividly represent what is meant by lines of power, which - in their way - also count.

To illustrate this double principle even better, I want to approach the whole thing via Lacan's Borromean Knot, a kind of PlayStation for psychoanalysts. Next to it there is an illustration (next page), but it is absolutely not necessary to understand all the details. One sees immediately that it is about three loops, which are connected in such a way that they all open, if one cuts only one. One also sees immediately the designations life, body and death, and also my Id *Rays* as the pictorial, imaginary, and the Id *Speaks* as the wordlike, symbolic, are drawn in. Again to the clarity: the imaginary, image-working is that what comes from the perception or looking drive (instinct) (drive), which rays therefore from the outside to the inside and from the inside to the outside.

It is a primary force as Freud said, the Id *Speaks*, on the other hand, comes from the expressive or speaking drive (instinct), which goes as an auditory component from the outside to the inside and as an expressing oneself from the inside to the outside. Both forces are in combination to something that Lacan attributed to the mathematicians. It is the real, that which counts, even if there is not yet a per-

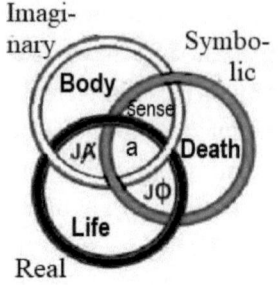

sonally counting person, that is, no mathematician; or is he there after all?

There have already been many scientists who have said that the world is built up mathematically in the end, and then the builder and creator would have been a mathematician. The mathematician Kronauer had once expressed himself for this reason in such a way: The calculations make the mathematicians, but the numbers made God. Well, this is such a saying which sounds so similar like that of "God's algorithm" with the so-called magic cube. God is here only hypothetically used, much more extreme and reality-addicted behaves the new best-selling author N. Harari in his book 'Homo Deus'.[38]

He doesn't want to make God an algorithmist or a number inventor, but immediately man to God. He also starts from counting, from the algorithms, these well-defined rules of action or calculation, which in his opinion come from the earthly-supernatural at the same time, but

---

[38] Harari, Y. N., Homo Deus, C. H. Beck (2017)

which one can imagine in their effect particularly well in the future of mankind. There they are namely present in the connection of bionics and the artificial intelligence, where undreamt-of possibilities open up for the human being. For until now, they had not been developed in this way and had not been seen in this way.

But Harari also looks back to the past in his book with this concept of the future, because algorithms have already functioned in the history of the world and in the lives of people in the past - even if not as complex as today and tomorrow. Right at the starting point, he claims that at the very beginning, namely, "in the animistic cosmos, everyone talked to everyone directly".[39] Algorithmically, of course, because verbal language did not yet exist. He also thinks that no one can prove that another has spirit as one does. The people are absorbed in the data flow, whether it is called spirit or matter, it doesn't matter, the algorithms think for both, for the material-biological and the spiritual-mental human being, identically and synchronously. The Other as such, the really Other, does not exist any more, at least he does not appear.

But recently it is feigned to us. In the 'Generative-Pretrained-Transformer' (GPT-3) a counterpart, a perfect Other, is presented to us by means of artificial intelligence. As a "text generator, it composes poems in the

---

[39] Harari, Y. N., Homo Deus, C. H. Beck (2017) S. 166 and following S. 129

style of Oskar Wilde and dramas in the language of Shakespeare. He understands guitar chord patterns, programs web pages as desired, and translates texts almost flawlessly into several languages. He can palaver with people about the weather and "discuss" climate policy.[40] It is celebrated as a technological wonder and feared as a monster. Because for sure he does not understand a joke as Freud has theorized. For he who understands a joke and can laugh about it has an unconscious such as only humans, speaking beings, have.

Conversely, but with the same statement that AI does not understand a joke. In a children's movie a robot was presented that a man had invented. He was convinced it was only a machine. His wife, however, said he was a human being. To test him, they told him a joke: a Catholic, a Protestant and a Jewish priest were to take a stand on the distribution of the money collected. The Catholic one said, we make a circle, throw the money up, what falls in the circle belongs to God, what falls outside belongs to the community. No, said the Protestant, we make a circle, throw the money up, what falls inside belongs to the community, what falls outside belongs to God. Finally, the Jewish one said, we make a circle, throw the money up, what falls down belongs to the community, what remains up belongs to God. Indeed, laughed the robot, he was therefore a man.

---

[40] Rodemann, J., Maschinen-Lyrik (Machines Lyric), SZ vom 24. 11. 2020, S. 13

Even more impressive is the story I myself experienced in my studies when my professor in neurology made a Freudian slip, a lapsus linguae. Instead of talking about competence, which he intended to do, he said compotence. Many students laughed. The good professor probably had problems with eroticism, but such an interpretation of the slip of the tongue would not occur to the AI. She would think that the second o in competence was a spelling or typographical mistake. The machines just don't have a sense of humor.

For a long time, there has been an attempt to have people and computers communicate on the inside of a room and separate people on the outside. Those in the outer area are supposed to find out whether they are talking to a human or to the supercomputer inside. Usually this only becomes clear after ten to fifteen minutes, because the machine is also tuned for bullshit and abstractions. Nowadays, 'deepfakes' are also used to perfectly fake movies, as we know since the Republicans' video about Obama with the aged face and the accurately recreated voice. As the AI expert Nina Schick reports, the Russians in particular are masters when it comes to the most deceitful lies and tricks.[41]

The fact that in a psychoanalysis one does not listen to the flow of data but to the revealing game of hidden eroticized words, and that one will communicate inter-

---

[41] Schick, N., Deepfakes, The Coming Infocalypse, Twelve Hachette Book Group (2020)

subjectively until it is clear that all those involved are more than algorithms because they recognize truth as cause, This is unknown to Harari and the GPT-3 entrepreneurs. Language is primarily not for communication, but for revelation, specifically for the revelation of hidden truths. Also in the universe is hidden not only the dark matter and dark energy, but the underlying truth of its complexity. Only when we know the truth about all these things, we can die with peace of mind. But this must be exercised in advance,

Harari remains in the constant game in which knowledge is always only programmatic and the question of its truth does not arise. For him, knowledge "does not constitute itself polar to the relation to the virtual position of a truth to be reached", but for Harari it is already there ready-made in the algorithms.[42] The words truth, love, eros, feeling and many other humanly so important terms do not appear at all in the register and text of his book, because he does not want to do anything with them. He is absolutely similar to the mischievous Sisyphus and his tricks and deceptive maneuvers.

"When an artificial intelligence says of itself", Harari writes, "that it is in a conscious state", there is no certain proof to the contrary. Virtual and real worlds are ultimately indistinguishable, and transcranial direct current brain stimulation can be used to show that everyone has

---

[42] Lacan, J., Seminar I, Walter (1986) S. 214

many egos and that the individual does not exist at all. Nevertheless, what Harari writes is not entirely silly. It immediately brings to mind again the outwitting of death by body-mind techniques that I mentioned earlier. Harari suggests that the idea of immortality has always been inherent in humans, and soon humans will become primordial anyway through modern technology and medicine. But the future lies in the transhumanism, in which humans become even God.

Harari thinks that man will become the data god, but who will actually survive when the question of immortality is taken up again. Woody Allen, when asked if he doesn't survive in his work, said, "I want to become immortal only by not dying myself". That's where the stupidity lies. By not wanting to die one will never cheat death, also the transhuman dataism man will not change anything. Because if the algorithms have ruled the man in the form of his unconscious up to now, then the transhuman dataism man, who can know everything and will be happy, because he can merge like before in God now in the data stream, will become reality indeed half consisting of biological, half consisting of technical substance.

But what will be the dying then? Will it be this trance-like going over, which is not yet a real going over at all, but only a seeing the other side of the own life, exactly this life in dying and not a life after death. It is only about an interface, a caesura, which one must at least - as it is in a meditation but also in certain phases of psycho-analysis - wander through half awake, work through, that's all it is. Dying does not always mean being dead. Conversely, one must practice dying in a tricky way, as Sisyphus did and as is possible in *Analytic Psychocatharsis*.

In this procedure, a first exercise serves to pass through the imaginary, the 'image-acting', i.e. the area in the Borromean knot which reaches from the 'body' to the 'life' and shows in its center an a filled with yellow a by me. For Lacan, the small a stands for the unconscious psychic 'object' of desire, that is, when someone is not yet aware that he has rivaled his father for his mother in an incestuous way. The capital A, on the other hand, stands for the Other, which I have already described several times as the significant, internalized Other. By means of control through the *formula-words*, in *Analytic Psychocatharsis* the a becomes the transitional object from the pictorial to the verbal, from the imaginary of the first exercise to the symbolic of the *pass-word* (of which I will mention two more) in the second exercise, in which A allows itself to be heard.

Lacan has entered death into the circular loop of the 'word-acting', the symbolic, the *Speaks*, which also counts, because it has contact with the real, and so has to do with the 'death of comprehension' I already mentioned above, which always accompanies general talk. I had also quoted Gamm, who wrote that all speaking and saying is struck by a residue of indeterminacy. Even if the patient in psychoanalysis has to 'free-associate', that is, to reveal oneself, give himself away, even to almost die of uttered embarrassments and stupidity, this death-like dropping is not enough to lead the therapy into its deepest layers. Something that is even still in syntax and grammar, even in the 'B(r)uchstaben (broken letters) themselves, prevents the final revelations and thus remains undetermined.[43] That is why psychoanalysts nowadays help themselves out of trouble with so-called 'enactments', i.e. artificial interventions, intervening remarks, invented interpretations, when they get stuck with the interpretation. But this does not help.

To achieve more one has to accept the snare of the imaginary, of the 'image-acting', of the Id *Rays*, into which Lacan has entered the body. Id also has contact with the symbolic, where it connects to meaning. Again, the reference to film (theater, performance, ritual, social events, etc.) is illuminating, for here image and word are used everywhere in close association, providing meaning and sense. Death is conveyed on the screen and in the book, but the closer their connection becomes, the closer the matter comes into play with the life of the real, that is, to what counts and where Lacan drew in the concept of life.

---

[43] Oudee Dünkelsbühler, U., Testimony and Writing: B(r)uchstaben (broken letters) an der Couch, Les Etats Généraux de la Psychanalyse (2001). The author alludes to Freudian slips of the tongue, where often only one letter is displaced, broken, but through which the repressed truth emerges.

But how can one now achieve more from this hullaba-loo, in terms of knowledge of the soul, therapy, self-practice, with which death can be outsmarted?

You have to start with the body that is entered in the circular loop of the imaginary. To this end, the following: At the heart of psychoanalysis is the concept of transference. In therapy, the client, patient, or whatever you want to call him, transfers meanings, from his past life or from completely different relationships, to the psychoanalyst by imputing a knowledge to him. He assumes that the therapist has acquired knowledge in his training, as at a university, with which he can fathom, recognize, even more or less see through his patient by means of a certain form of conversation. The psychoanalyst is therefore also called the 'transference object', that is, the hoard to which all the meanings can be transferred, so that they are kept there for the time being, but can also contribute something to the treatment and, through a kind of transformation, can finally be used for healing.

Transformation means that the therapist has to dissolve this transference, because it is not adequate, it is not appropriate, it is just another kind of illness or, in other words, the disorder to be treated has only shifted to another one, which, however, is better suited to recognize the mechanisms of being ill and thus to dissolve them. Therefore, professionally, one speaks of the transference neurosis, into which the patient crosses over from the neurosis he is suffering from. Now only the *Rays* of the body image and the *Speaks* of death are present in order to gain life from it.

Therefore, when the patient asks what is actually wrong with him, the 'transference object' psychoanalyst answers, for example, that this question probably has to do with the fact that the patient's mother never really acknowledged him or that she overprotected him. Although behind this shifting answer is the fact that he, the therapist, cannot give the recognition either, and that there must not be the over-bothering, the patient nevertheless reacts by now telling something about the relationship with his mother. He brings up all kinds of stories, memories surface, feelings are awakened, etc., and after many, many hours it becomes clear that the recognition must come from him, the patient himself. No one can confirm who one is, and so basically the psychoanalyst must also have confirmed to himself at some point that he is a psychoanalyst, that he can practice this profession. Admittedly, he will have read Freud, put himself on the couch with the teaching analyst, and attended seminars. In the end, however, he has to invent himself to do it.

One cannot become a psychoanalyst by means of an official exam. At some point one must have recognized the inner logical structure of one's own unconscious and feel that one can get involved with others, listen to them, take in everything with oneself as an 'object of transmission', in other words: as a sewage treatment plant. And then one should also be able to formulate an interpretation only from these two forces, signifiers, image-word-acting (Id *Rays* and *Speaks*) and their entanglements. The stone of Sisyphus, which is loaded with the unconscious desires, longings, urges and phantasms, is lifted up to the solution plateau again and again, until the patient leaves the therapy hour again, after which he lands at the bottom again.[44]

But like the aforementioned patient who one day feels that his mother could not have been the person who could have given him recognition or who could have given him overprotection, today's psychoanalyst also feels that the treatment threatens to fail when psychic transferences can no longer be properly grasped, when they can no longer be traced back to relationships that can be objectified, and when he has to resort to the 'enactments' mentioned above. But the calculation does not quite work out because - as I have already shown - psychoanalysis remains bound to the one-sided emphasis on the side of the symbolic and cannot include the imaginary enough and does not count the real enough.

That is why sometimes a figure like Sisyphus counts more than all the gray theory. In his new book 'An Odyssey' the author D. Mendelsohn has also tried it with

---

[44] In this regard, Freud also spoke of "infinite analysis", which also culminates in the fact that no therapist has ever completely finished his analysis.

Odysseus.[45]A professor of ancient philology is holding a seminar on Homer's Odyssey. His old father, who still had to work out his studies himself and became a mathematician, is also a participant in the seminar. A tension develops between father and son that has always existed covertly. The father demands exact science, the son insists on the well-told story, which, even if it is not entirely true (se non è vero), is nevertheless well told (è bene raccontato), as an old Italian proverb says. The father/son and the woman/man relationship have the same structure, so the solution was.

Home, family, identity, all themes are discussed between father and son after the seminar on a sea voyage in the footsteps of Ulysses, with the ancient hero always the mediating symbol that ultimately clarifies and mends the relationship between the two. It always takes only two characters and a third, all-encompassing being to answer completely the question of what man is. In the case of the novel mentioned above, it is the figure of Odysseus. In him, the father/son conflict seems to be absent, but it is only shifted to the man/woman relationship. In his bid for the beautiful Helen, Odysseus' had no chance, but he got the second of those female luxury creatures of Greek antiquity, Penelope, which was not bad for the revival of the hero.

---

[45] Mendelsohn, D., Eine Odyssee, (An Odyssey), Siedler publishing (2019).

The Italian writer A. Moravia in his book 'The Contempt' has given an attempt in the sense of a psychoanalytic interpretation - at least he called it so - of Odysseus and Penelope's married life, which turns out differently from the classical myth, in which the two are bound to each other in a monstrous pathos of fidelity. Moravia parallels the relationship of the novel's main protagonists, Ricardo and his wife Emilia, with that of Odysseus and Penelope. Ricardo is supposed to write a screenplay about the two ancient spouses, finally, because so far the screenwriter has not achieved much in life. But the German director, who is finally to shoot the film about Odysseus and Penelope, wants a different story than that of the hero Odysseus and his wife, who is faithful to the point of no return, and claims the following:

Even at Penelope's marriage there were already the many suitors, some of whom were to play a major role even later, after Odysseus' return from Troy. After an initially positive marriage, Penelope was soon annoyed by the way Odysseus dealt with these early suitors and those who remained after the wedding. Odysseus let them, did not take a stand against them and treated them waxy and half-hearted and had not driven them away. On the contrary, he thought he had to constantly show only how great it was that he represented the intellectual and eigually civilized, while Penelope was still retarded in the original affective of the closed Greek agrarian society.

Penelope began to despise more and more her arrogant and vain life partner. She, who considered herself the emotional and not inferior to her cousin Helena, increasingly rejected Odysseus. Finally, however, Odysseus could no longer stand it at home. He therefore gladly took the opportunity to go to war with Troy. And after the end of the same - according to the director in Moravia's book - there was no ten-year long odyssey, but Odysseus postponed the final return again and again in order to be able to enjoy himself with other women. He may have thought himself noble, but he unconsciously felt prey again and again to the 'marital aversion' that weighed on his relationship with Penelope like a curse. In the end, however, he always overcame this and returned home, chasing away the suitors and regaining Penelope's trust.

In Moravia's novel, the protagonist Ricardo now realizes that this, now modern version of the ancient drama, totally mirrors his own relationship with his wife Emilia. Although he clings to the hero and fidelity genre of the ancient Odysseus saga to the very end and considers his own marriage to be similarly noble, Emilia rejects him just as much and leaves him as Penelope did with Odysseus in Moravia's novel - but for ever. A revival is no longer possible. Now, one could say that the actual, overarching truth of the story probably lies somewhere between the ancient and modern versions. Neither was Odysseus the great hero he has always been handed down as, nor did he suffer from a 'marital aversion complex', as Moravia tries to make us believe. But then who was he really?

Neither the father/son nor the woman/man relationship can solve totally the basic problem that appears in the ancient myths from Sisyphus to Prometheus to Odysseus, and so cannot revive the man of today. One has to solve it in oneself and for this one needs also this third, this third figure, this 'trialogical practice', but no longer in such a fairy-tale and dazzlingly equipped form.[46] It needs a "body without shape", Lacan thinks, and so even in the psycho-analyst's consulting room, in the middle between him and the patient, there still sits the spirit of Freud, or the creator of the word, the juggler of meanings, the unconscious. 'linguistic-crystalline' way. 'L'Autre, as Lacan says, the Other in and outside us, who cannot be satisfied with great stories.

In the sexual - and in the dramas of antiquity it is always about Eros, which is, after all, abused by Zeus, the father of the gods, in an extremely promiscuous way, and which, as already mentioned, is only an illusory relationship, the solution cannot be found. But also in all conventional religions, literatures, sciences and wisdoms it cannot be found. 'Wanted reformers not of others, but of themselves' is an old saying. One can only find the solu-

---

[46] The concept of 'trialogue' as a contrast to the conventional and only seemingly perfect dialogue was developed by my teaching analyst, O. Count Wittgenstein. I have reported on this in detail in my book 'teadrunken'.

tion by means of the identity and *pass-words*, the sewage treatment plant interpretations through one's own going within.

5. The Sisyphus Complex

Now there is an improvement of the situation just by taking in the body especially in the way of the body image, which Lacan has entered into the circular loop of the imaginary. The body is therefore connected with the pictorial, the *Rays*, the 'pictorial reality', because it consists of anatomical images, which one does not feel in their material precision, but of which one always has an unconscious image in oneself. As the French psychoanalyst F. Dolto proved, the body image is mainly composed of three parts, the basal, dynamic and erotic body image. She thus best shows that the body together with its ego is composed of imaginary-real objects whose number can go far beyond three and thus accesses the symbolic-real.[47]

The lion cannot count to three, let alone beyond, as Lacan once remarked at the London Zoo, where the lion was surrounded by three lionesses. Outraged listeners protested. The lion would know perfectly well that he had three lovers, after all, he can see that, and moreover he probably smells it, whereas man needs a slide rule to understand his love relationships. But in a purely arith-

---

[47] Dolto, F., The Unconscious Image of the Body, Quadriga Verlag (1999). The term image here goes a bit beyond the purely imaginary, and when it is a matter of more than three images, the word must also help to capture the real, the effectively real.

metical sense, Lacan was right. The lion doesn't count, he doesn't add, from three on there are simply many for him and so the lionesses are not jealous either, because - according to Lacan - for sexual jealousy it is necessary to be able to count.[48] There may be some truth in this.

The body and its ego can get lost in the imaginary, in the Id *Rays*, but counting, telling, the narrative - as modern linguists and sociological describers of human beings like to say today - brings the transference moment, the Id *Speaks*, into human relations. I have already mentioned how the psychoanalysts reckon with it: because you impute something to someone every now and then, you transfer something to him, something quite different from what you impute and tell him. The psychoanalyst R. Lombardi - it is always the unknown protagonists who have the most exciting ideas - writes in his publications about the fact that besides the therapist as an 'object of transference', above all the body itself, built up in its imaginary variety, is suitable as an 'object of transference'. For Lombardi, the body is a *Rays/Speaks* combination to which one can communicate something and which also responds to it.

It is, after all, the body with its libidinous projections far beyond its material limits, which - since its ears cannot be closed as Lacan noted - must absorb all sound images (noises, words, sighs, cries, etc.) and mix them with all

---

[48] Lacan, J., Seminaire Nr. IX, Staferla, S. 202 (20. 6. 1962)

the pictorial parts within itself, so that a complex unconscious is created. This *Rays/Speaks* - unconscious can thus listen excellently, but it can also give out interpretations such as symptoms, failures, slips of the tongue, but also distressing and illuminating images, misjudgements and visionary insights, flashes of thoughts, memorials, heraldics, art. I have from the B(r)uchstabensammler (the broken letter collector as mentioned an expression of the psychoanalyst O. Dünklesbühler for the unconscious), because there the words are often pieced and broken and so issued.

U. Karacaoğlan writes in a book review about Lombardi and his thesis of 'transference to the body' as follows: "According to Lombardi, transference to the analyst and transference to the body complement each other, creating a double and parallel transference of both participants to their own corporeality, which in a crucial way enables communication within the analytic couple. . . Lombardi calls this "working through the body-soul connection.[49] This achieves a therapy that operates close to the body as a *Rays/Speaks* combination and is closer to reality, which is also possible in *Analytic Psychocatharsis* and is even the focus here. Here the unconscious of the body gives a direct answer by means of the *pass-words*.

---

[49] Lombardi, R., Der Körper in der analytischen Sitzung (The Body in Analytic Session) , in Mauss-Hanke: Internationale Psychoanalyse, Bd. 4 (2009)

Thus, the unconscious is not only word-like-lexical as in the classical psychoanalytic approach, but also body-image-like-creative and rhythmic-musical, as the psychoanalysts S. Leikert, R. Zwiebel and some other authors have demonstrated.[50] In particular, if one gives the body in a relaxed posture a small order-instrument into the hand as for example the yes also pictorial *formula-words*, this unconscious can give deep and nevertheless clear interpretations of itself, as it was for me the "What offers Sisyphus". About Sisyphus exists a vast number of pictures and books in this regard.

He is portrayed as cheerful, as persevering, as 'my brother' and, above all, again and again as the one who ultimately draws great profit from failure, in that he is always depicted as the strong one who has to roll a huge stone upwards. The stone can never have been as large as it is usually depicted; it is more a symbol, a painting and a revelation. That is why the conclusion of most commentaries, pictures and statements on the fate of Sisyphus is not to stop in the face of failure and not to let the negative sides of life get you down. But that is not enough in terms of conveying the truth. It needs a psychological-cultural differentiation and a psychoanalytical interpretation.

---

[50] Leikert, S., Die vergessene Kunst (The forgotten art), Psychoanalyse und Musik, Psychosozial Verlag (2005)

The only book that is still quite interesting in connection with this mythical figure is the treatise of the psychiatrist A. Marneros, who attests Sisyphus a compulsive disease. Sisyphus is chronically obsessive-compulsive, the rolling up of the stone is a purely compulsive action, which, as is well known, must always be repeated unconsciously and is always accomplished again, because the conscious insight that the performed action is nonsensical does not help. The cigarette smoker also knows that his addiction is harmful, and he wants to give it up, but he continues to smoke, just as Sisyphus always drags his stone back up the hill. Maneros thinks that compulsive acts are usually expressions of a defence against anxiety, and so many rituals, repeated gestures, and cults that serve a regulation of interpersonal relations are also considered as compulsive neurotics. Freud therefore considered most religious practices with their monotonous recitations, acts of sacrifice, symbolism, and incantation to be pathological.

Now one must admit that the myth of Sisyphus fits very well to the obsessive-compulsive neurotic. So it has nothing to do with the happy man who loves his stone and defies the gods as Camus did it. The one who does his work contemptuously and masters his fate heroically. Always repeating the same activity distracts one from ugly thoughts and depression and gives life a semblance of structure that is better to bear than to expose oneself to the darkness of a fear or negativity. In a way, everyone struggles with this, even nowadays. Aren't the 'doers' who constantly have to do something, who are miserable if they can't work, watch the sports show, or travel, to name just three examples, of which there are actually thousands, modern Sisyphuses in the sense of obsessive-compulsive disorder?

Sisyphus punishes himself with his hard work, nobody forced him to do it. But people often first try to put the blame not on themselves, but somewhere else. Many of my patients said, why do I of all people have this or that disease, I haven't done anything wrong! But if you ask, you will find out that they did not eat right, did not exercise enough, thought too wrongly, slept too much, lived too addicted, loved too little and what else they did negatively. But especially in the field of neuroses and personality disorders one wants to see the causes in diseased dispositions or devastating environmental conditions, which does not always have to be unjustified, because such superpositions of causes cannot be excluded even in Sisyphus' story.

Nevertheless, why should he not have been somewhat compulsively neurotic, but in the end the essence of his character did not consist in that. He has taken up the fight with the gods, psychoanalytically one would say: the fight with his 'drive fate' und his therapists (Zeus, Thanatos, the women, Persephone, Ixion and others), without whom his life is unthinkable.[51] In general, I have

---

[51] To Ixion more on the next page.

to expand the narratives about Sisyphus here, because they also lead psychoanalytically into a much broader area of human psycho-physical existence. I say psycho-physical, because the discussions go deep into the unconscious, namely to the origin of the same in the primordial repression so postulated by Freud. It is the first repression, a psycho-energetic anticathexis elementarily establishing itself to the developing psyche, which remains permanent and can never reach the conscious. The concept is not completely clarified until today, but it becomes more comprehensible if one looks at the full story of Sisyphus and listens to the arguments of the psychoanalyst Judith Le Soldat about it.

Before still the following: I have already indicated the sun titan and the creation myths. The well-known mythologist Ranke-Graves writes again: "The 'treacherous' stone of Sisyphus was originally a sun disk; the hill is the vault of heaven, a well-known image. The existence of the Corinthian sun cult is well documented. . . Moreover, in Tartarus, Sisyphus is always placed next to Ixion. Ixion's wheel of fire is also a sun symbol". Ixion was thus a nefarious hero comparable to Sisyphus. They met in Hades and exchanged stories about their fates. Ixion feigned a grand wedding with the moon goddess Dia, but lured his father-in-law into a deadly trap. Later, he even tried to seduce Hera, wife of the father god Zeus, but Zeus surprised him and had him tied to a wheel of fire forever. An ancient thriller.

The Corinthian people "are said to have sprung from mushrooms: mushrooms were the ritual igniter of Ixion's wheel of fire, and the sun god demanded human burnt offerings at the beginning of his year.[52] Antikleias' seduction [as already described by Sisyphus] is also probably derived from a picture showing the marriage of Helios, the sun god, to Aphrodite. . . Sisyphus' over-listing of Hades probably refers to a refusal by the saint-king to abdicate at the end of his reign".[53] Ranke-Graves, a mythologist, also describes that later myth writers were hostile to Sisyphus and spoke ill of him for not encouraging Hellenic settlements in his Corinthian kingdom, that is, in the narrow place separating Attica from the Peloponnese. Thus, ancient and modern mythic representations intersect in extreme ways with politics and personal conflicts. Moreover: mushrooms could have to do with alkaloids, psychedelic substances.

Ixion was himself a major 'holy king' and moon god. It was common for these early rulers to even dub themselves Zeus, and so it is thought that Dia himself was considered identical with Hera, but this was opposed by the Olympian priests, and so they too put negative lore into the world. But who were Sisyphus and his companions really? In order to answer this question better, I take

---

[52] As in early Central America, the mushrooms and their active ingredients were probably mescaline, psilocybin and similar hallucinogens, which - ritually ingested - triggered the creation myth.

[53] An act still common among autocratic politicians today.

the remarks of the psychoanalyst Le Soldat to help, who vividly criticized Freud's conception of the Oedipus myth as a basic human complex by taking apart and picking apart Freud's initial dream (the dream of 'Irma's injection') in detail. Freud, she argued, had only used the Oedipus story to provide himself with an excuse, a psychic defense, so as not to have to face those violent sexual and sadistic impulses that dwell in the elemental unconscious. Thus Le Soldat has completely turned Freud's theory upside down and plumbed into the erotic-aggressive, which fits the Sisyphus story.

Macabre and curious, she describes how it is not the Oedipus complex and castration anxiety that are the central elements of Freudian therapy. Rather, the focus is on the sphinx standing between the homicidal jealousy toward the father and the eros infatuation with the mother in the Oedipus saga.[54] She is a woman and mother figure endowed with male sexuality, which at the beginning of life plunges the still immature child's soul into unsolvable conflicts. Towards her, the child develops libidinous-aggressive strivings by means of unconscious fantasy formations, which block each other because both protagonists, man/father and woman/mother, let the different sexual organs act imaginary at the same time. Uncon-

---

[54] Le Soldat, J., Eine Theorie menschlichen Unglücks, Trieb, Schuld, Phantasie (A theory of human misfortune, Drive, Guilt and Phantasy)Fischer Sozialwissenschaft (1994)

sciously a castration lust comes about, the male child for example wants to rob this sphinx-like mother-woman - everything still to be understood unconsciously - of the organ of her perpetual enjoyment (which is indeed autochthonous, but now has a male-phallic character), but it threatens itself with so much own sadism at the same time with fear of punishment and confusion.

In order to arrive at psychoanalytic interpretations at all, however, Le Soldat has to elicit corresponding fantasies from her patients, which seems a bit manipulative. I think that Le Soldat's psychoanalysis as therapy is only valid in special cases. But as a theoretic contribution Le Soldat's reflections are valuable, because the crucial interface between myth and reality (and that is what Sisyphus is all about), which in her case is approached aggressively and at the same time with great libidinous and almost monster-like phantasms, clearly sets the inner-psychic conflicts in motion. Prehistory and unconscious, thus enter into a close connection, which was certainly already Freud's starting point and also fits the devastating lust and consumer addictions and wars of our time.

But Freud did not mention Sisyphus even once, although he was otherwise taken with so many figures of Greek mythology. Prometheus, Odysseus, Uranos, Pegasus, Oedipus, Zeus, Orpheus and many others have their say. Doesn't the fact that Sisyphus remains so disregarded by Freud have something to do with the fact that his story reaches into the creation myths, and thus has meaning for the most precarious depths of the soul, while Oedipus is already a more modern figure of the Greek dramas? The Oedipus myth could lend itself well to the treatment of neurosis, but the Sisyphus myth would also capture more complex, deeper psychological structures. In any case, the reality mixed with such confusing stories in the myth of Sisyphus was highly explosive and still is today: not only among neurotics, but also among potentates, scientists, financial jugglers, power politicians, warlords, rapists, corrupt civil servants, paedophiles, Internet liars, and a thousand others so deeply entangled in the unconscious.[55]

It is the so encrusted power-, money-, as well as the narcissistic and ego-addicted structures that should be treated. But it behaves like in the cabaret, where those who are ridiculed and highballed don't go there at all. They don't have to fear the laughter, because they leave it to the decent people who have nothing else to laugh about. Sisyphus would be a good advisor, because he was not concerned with money and power, but with the symbolism of values, with the respect and dignity that is denied to the simple worker not because of the monetary value of Warren Buffet's billions, but because the financial

---

[55] If I have included scientists here, it is because new genetic techniques such as the so-called check-point inhibitors are so promoted and praised in cancer therapy, even though they have significant side effects almost 100% of the time. Wouldn't you rather keep your cancer?

difference is so insanely great that it chaotically determines the symbolism of values, of dignity. If a politician wears gold watches costing tens of thousands on his wrist, he can afford it monetarily and personally, but for him as a guideline maker it is disastrous.

Discussing this, however, is not why I am writing about Sisyphus. Mainly it is about dying and death, and this also with regard to the psychoanalysts, who all die so badly. Already Freud died in such a terrible way, he suffered for years from oral cavity cancer probably caused by his life-long massive cigar consumption. J. Kollbrunner has reported in detail how many unhelpful operations Freud had to undergo and how in the end only a few morphine injections could put an end to his suffering and life.[56] Bettelheim immediately put a plastic bag over his head, Fenichel died already at the age of 48 from overweight, exhaustion, struggle for recognition and other things more and even Lacan, whom I appreciate, did not have a good death. Still in the sixties he had mocked students who did not know what aphasia was, but fell ill with it himself in combination with other neurological disorders and in the end also suffered from intestinal cancer, which was probably related to too much good wine and exclusive food (too much meet).

---

[56] Kollbrunner, J., Der kranke Freud (The sick Freud), Klett-Cotta (2001)

Psychoanalysis has so far not contributed much to the management of death and dying. While in philosophy and even in everyday life this topic plays a major role, in psychoanalysis it is only "latently known".[57] The psychoanalysts believe that Eros is immortal - it is, but only in the concretistic narrowness of the *Rays / Speaks*, in the closest combination of the looking and speaking drive (instinct), which can be well imagined on the basis of the myth of Sisyphus and also worked out on the basis of the *Analytic Psychocatharsis*.[58] I do not describe this procedure in this book in all details, only in a short appendix I have summarized the essentials of the practice. The most effective way to do justice to the Sisyphus complex is the method in which the soul close to the body, and not only the therapist, is the 'transference object'.

For ultimately it is the dying of the body that is so frightening to people and with which they now expose their souls to mortal danger. People simply do not see enough how to die well. There are no role models for this, and so the only salvation can lie in making oneself a role model in this respect. One must practice dealing with death, one must not just let it stand in the corner as a spectre of terror. I have already mentioned that depres-

---

[57] Biermann, C., Psychoanalytiker und Tod (Psychoanalyst and Death), E-Book (2006)

[58] In close alloy of the eros-life drive with the death drive - according to Freud's theory - man does not become immortal.

sion and despair are also a way of practicing dying. But why let it come so far. In the process of *Analytic Psychocatharsis* one can practice dealing with death and thus outsmart it - at least to a large extent - by overcoming the body as *Rays/Speaks* as the guarantor of life.

This happens not only by copying in the cathartic regression of the procedure the same process as it happens in dying. It happens above all through the *pass-words* that enable one to converse with death like Sisyphus or the Brandner Kasper. For whether one calls the Other the personified unconscious, or the inner-psychic instance close to the superego, or the Lacanian word-real Other, or even death as a conundrum mirror of life, it doesn't really matter. When spoke with the devil, because he - as he said - could talk with him better than with God, the same is meant. One must be able to talk with oneself in the form of also the negative, also the negation.

6. A Psychoanalysis for All

I want to emphasize once again that classical psychoanalysis is predominantly based on the verbal, the symbolic, the Id *Speaks*, and that the image-acting, the imaginary is thereby a bit neglected. The patient must speak whatever comes to his mind, the analyst must put this into interpretative words. Together they 'speak', so to say, the result of their speech relationship. Even pictures in dreams are not interpreted primarily according to their pictorial character, but according to their word-sound character. When one of the patients said to Freud that he had dreamed of Van Houten cocoa, Freud asked, "when does the mother (German: haut) chop"? And indeed, the patient thought of a story about it that was meaningful. Even when Freud seemed to interpret an image, e.g. a theater room, he interpreted it as the place of the marriage ceremony, but here, too, the word 'wedding theater' probably played more of a role.

Now this doesn't always work out so well that the literal meaning can be extracted from the images in such a sophisticated way. Certainly, a theater in a dream is not always indication of the wedding, and even if it is, it still needs to be clarified what is problematic about the wedding. The patient must bring further associations, which may even lead away from the actual subject again. In the *pass-words* I have created, it is much easier and more direct to reach what it is about, because the pictorial is already processed in them, the imaginary comes to light already successful combined with the symbolic from the unconscious. Yes, the emphasis of the *Analytic Psychocatharsis* lies from the beginning more on the pictorial, imaginary, the Id *Rays*, and that is why the *pass-word* must sometimes be retarranged.

In every meditation, memories, thoughts of all kinds of events arise, which in a certain way are always accompanied by images. The meditator pushes these aside, he keeps in the *Analytic Psychocatharsis* only the 'Rays-Point', an elementary image pattern, a topological form, the core of one's own body image in the (inner) eye. By core one can also understand the body images mentioned by F. Dolto, which in the catharsis, in the cathartic part of the first exercise, are superimposed or pushed into each other. It is precisely this that gives rise to the liberating, gratifying aspect of this exercise, because the majority of body images as distinguished by Dolto only express the dividedness of man, which is essential for him, but need not be so.[59] If one could permanently unite the body images, one would be beatified like God.

But I don't know anyone who has ever succeeded in doing that. In fact, in most other meditations, in the

---

[59] A large part of the psychic split already comes about with the human being by the fact that his strong language-relatedness has separated him from the nature-relatedness. The philosopher Hegel therefore said: "The word is murder of the thing", and one must get away from this murder.

background of these images there is the image of the meditation teacher, which actually interferes with the merging of the body images. In Christian meditations it is the image of Christ, in yoga or Zen Buddhism it is the yoga or Zen teacher, who sometimes appears in a direct vision-hallucination, as Yogananda writes.[60] Such image-appearances are admittedly a detour, for one remains attached to these images often called 'astral' and also to the mythical-magical-mystical themes associated with them. So the psychoanalyst remains preferably involved in the symbolic, the meditator in the imaginary, but both are important and therefore have to be brought together.

The meditation teacher Sant Kirpal Singh, whom I knew personally, used a clever way out of this problem. The wrinkles of his forehead showed an OM-sign, which has played an important role in Hinduism since ancient times. If at all an image appearance is necessary, one should concentrate on such a minimal ray design, he said. I also referred to this in my book 'Yoga and Psychoanalysis', as I later remarked, that the OM-sign and different topologies have similarities to each other (see illustration next side).

However, these are only analogous representations, which I think have only one meaning, to express the most limited, concise appearance of the Id *Rays* as can

---

[60] Paramahansa Yogananda, Autobiography of a Yogi, Self Real. Fellowship (1998), wherein the author meditates on the vision of his teacher after his death.

be seen, for example, in the three rings of the Borromean knot or in the looping of the Möbius strip. In no case fixed pictures have a sense, no matter what they show. The catharsis can already be achieved with the experience of a brightness (lucidity), and even better with this body image overlay, which can lead to a bodily 'trickle-through' feeling.

The Borromean knot (top right), Boy's plane (top left), the Möbius strip (bottom left) and the OM sign (bottom right), whose comparable similarities in psychoanalytic topology and yoga are shown here.

In the imaginary, one needs such a concise clue, an "apearance with importance" as the philosopher W. Seitter said,[61] something impressive, significant, in other words: "The first symbols, the natural symbols emerged from a certain number of significant images - from the image of the human body, from the image of a number of clearly visible objects such as the sun, the moon and some others. And this is what gives human language its weight, its driving force and its emotional vibration".[62] The most significant image that exists is the Id *Rays* (the

[61] Seitter, W., Physik des Daseins (Physics oft he Existance), Sonderzahl (1997) S. 213-14
[62] Lacan, J., Seminar II, Walter (1980) S.388

lucidity), which is at the same time the mainspring for the Id *Speaks*.

The imaginary, pictorial signifier, the *Rays*, is thus clearly separated/connected in relation to the symbolic, word-like, the *Speaks*. One has to put it this way. Freud said that the basic drives are autonomous and yet also closely linked. This is a very simple and clear statement. It is also what applies to the practice of *Analytic Psychocatharsis*, where in the first exercise one pays attention to that which somehow has the character of an Id *Rays*. To this fits well the one side of the nature of Sisyphus, when one has to imagine him as the Lord of the Sun Disk, as a relic of the Sun God. In this form he represents light, warmth, love and elixir of life, maybe not more, but equally different than Camus claimed with his word of Sisyphus as the "happy man". Perhaps he was, but that does not characterize his being. After all, he had a lot to say and even negotiated with Tartarus.

In many meditations it is suggested to focus on an 'inner light', which is really purely mystical. If I bring Sisyphus into play here, it is only as a human measure, as a suggestion to his sun-warming Eros and to his brightness-giving 'inner touch'.[63] With this notion and that of a ray,

---

[63] Heller-Roazen, D., Der innere Sinn, Archäologie eines Gefühls, (The Inner Touch, archeology of an inner feeling)fischer wissenschaft (2012). The author means by this a feeling from within, a 'being radiated, shivered through' from one's own body image.

however illuminating and 'penetrating' the body image, I definitely do justice to psychoanalytic science (Lacan's 'ultrasubjective radiance', oscillation point in the concave mirror of the brain or the body images, etc.), and can thus add that one does not have to actively, wilfully, concentrate on it.[64] For this Point of the *Rays* represents nothing else than the primary process of the perceptive or viewing drive, as one of the two basic forces, drives, principles, and thus represents a psychoanalysis for all.

Because the classical psychoanalysis is a method for the elites (young, rich, intellectual, as it has always been said). It can be available only to a few, because the analytic therapist cannot treat more than two or three hundred patients in his whole life. But the *Analytic Psychocatharsis* is addressed to all (a minimum of education is necessary). If one must think of Sisyphus on the one hand as a descendant of the sun god, on the other hand he represents the rebellious, original human being, the left-liberal, whom the rulers, the right-autocrats, do not want or vice versa. This struggle between left and right, between master and servant (Hegel's dialectic of history), extroverted doers and introverted meditators, has

---

[64] Again, it is the phenomenon that everyone knows from a moving piece of music, when it 'trickles' down one's back. It is an atavistic experience, that is something that played an important role in the communication of the early humans, but is only given to the modern man by extraordinary experiences. The starting point for this 'trickling' phenomenon is the reflection point in the brain, as I have shown it on page 59.

been going on for millennia. Sisyphus overcomes this division, which is destroying human society again today, by expressing the rebellious, fortunate side in addition to the light-giving, love and warmth of the divine. He even argues with death and has good arguments every time.

Because I bring these good arguments to bear in the second exercise, the practitioner does not fall into this division, but rather dissolves it in himself as the Unifying Subject. The *pass-words* are really the best arguments, because they come from an unconscious self and yet are linguistically composed. In conventional psychoanalysis, something similar to *pass-words* also ultimately come about, they are the 'transference interpretations'. [65] They are only much more cumbersome to reach. Freud, in one of his last articles "Die Ich-Spaltung im Abwehrprozess" (The Ego-Spitting in the Defence Process) also describes this phenomenon of splitting and 'transference interpretation', which are handled more simply in *Analytic Psychocatharsis*.

He tells the story of a psychic split once on the basis of a three- or four-year-old child. He said that normally, with

---

[65] An interpretation of the pure conversational material is not sufficient to interpret the unconscious of the patient; the therapist must give an interpretation out of the transference, that is, out of the function that is assumed of him in the form of knowledge and other relations. Moreover, the interpretation must contain an equivoc, on which I will comment in a moment.

regard to the early childhood (as opposed to pubertal) onanism occurring at this age, the parents' threat to the boy that his penis will be cut off has no particular effect. The little boy knows perfectly well that this is not really going to happen, even if he is a bit frightened. But it is different in the case described by Freud.

This boy had "become acquainted with the female genitals through seduction on the part of an older girl", Freud writes, and so the boy saw that the girl had actually been castrated and had a kind of wound there, where a penis belongs after all. [66]Now the said threat had a completely different effect. Because the visual, the show, the exciting imaginary (Id *Rays*) coincides with the word, with the symbolic threat (Id *Speaks*), it comes - according to Freud - to the real castration fear, which the child solves in this case by splitting: "He created a substitute for the missing penis of the woman, namely a fetish. In this way he had denied reality, but saved his own penis". Well.

Is it really always the case that the first sight of the female genital turns out to be so exciting? If you look at the painting of the early impressionist G. Courbet 'The Origin of the World' in the Musée d'Orsay in Paris, you might also be a little surprised. Because there it is about this ominous genital in a somewhat provocative form. I myself have had quite different experiences. I remember that at the age of maybe six another boy explained to me

---

[66] Freud, S., GW, Band XVII, Fischer (1999)

that the girls had two 'rolls', we only had one. At that time, in the unimmediate post-war period, there existed only strongly center-notched rolls, and that, my playmate probably thought, is what the bottom looks like, but also - somewhat smaller - what the girl's vulva looks like. So the girls have two of these significant features, we boys only one.

This evaluation made sense to me immediately, even if the ambiguity of the whole thing became clear to me only much later: first, that the girls who had been devalued in Freud's story as castrated boys came off much better here, because we boys would have only one of these sex symbols, but the girls even two. Second, that the playmate speaks of rolls probably had to do with the fact that this conversation between me and the other boy took place in the aforementioned immediate post-war period, where a roll was a high commodity, indeed the most valuable thing of all. We were not terribly hungry, but a fresh roll was something great that was somehow constantly present in our souls. I was now wholly enlightened by my playmate, and this, moreover, in such vivid and pleasant, if quite un-Freudian, form. Nevertheless, Freud's story has its full meaning and also represents a good example of the concept of splitting.

The split is something quite universal, it also exists between the therapist and his patient, between the sexes, between psyche and body and also between two different parts of the soul. That is why it is advantageous to use the body as an object of transference, as it happens in meditation, even if the meditation teacher also gets something of the transference, this positive attitude. Sometimes one speaks of the love of transference, and that one turns to one's body in this positive way also causes it to give back something corresponding. Of course, the body does not ask back what else comes to mind about this or that aspect, in order to then give a ready-to-print interpretation like the therapist. It mediates in a more immediate way, in that the resonance organ, the echo organ of the body in the unconscious, suddenly begins to articulate itself, and thus gives the passwords their stringency and directness.

I have just spoken above of the similarity of the transference interpretation, because here also an echo phenomenon occurs or should occur (what was called equivocation in footnote 62). "The drives", Lacan says, "are the echo in the body because there is a saying", a syllable, verb, phrase resonance. Because the ear cannot be closed, everything gathers in the echo organ as a buzz of voices, which then finds its way out in the constant chatter, in the free associations and also in the *pass-words*, which now finally convey what wants to be said, namely the truth.

Between the ego and the body it is also about a 'loosened, made-up love', an auto-eroticism is not meant. But that the body as *Rays/Speaks* not only gives biological life, but also contributes something to the unconscious,

Freud often emphasized. After all, he conceived of the basic drives as body-related, although he was not clear whether hormones or functions of the nervous system play a role here. However, Freud did not want to know about the body-related things that occurred in the course of his therapy experiments with hypnosis. When treated by suggestion, patients lost themselves to the sound of Freud's voice. They regarded the hypnotizing therapist too much as a divinely acting physician, gave themselves over to a dependence intoxication on his voice and divine presence, and thus believed they were walking in otherworldly spheres. For a serious therapy the profession was then flattened and the chance for a visible opening of the unconscious was lost.

This danger does not exist with the body as an 'object of transference'. It is not a matter of autoerotism, if one surrenders oneself to the *Rays / Speaks* and waits for the cathartic feeling that proves this constriction (défiles signifiantes) of the two basic forces, as it is the case in sleep. Only in sleep the necessary consciousness is missing. The catharsis, however, is helpful in the transition to the *pass-words*. It gives the feeling of certainty, which does not mean scientific precision. Such a certainty only comes about through the *pass-words* and their interpretation, which is why I am quoting an example again here, because authentic case descriptions are best suited for understanding the procedure.

Thus once one of my test persons heard the following saying: "She already has her work clothes". In any case, it sounded to him quite clearly like that from the depths, and he knew immediately what it was about. By 'she' was meant the girlfriend he had known for some time and intended to marry. And the term 'work clothes' didn't make any problem either, he told me, because she just consisted of nothing, that is, only of her bare skin, of the entire surface of her sex appeal. As much as the occurrence of such a *pass-word* astonished him in general, he was also shocked by the ironic, almost mocking truth of this saying, which he felt was a thought he himself would never think like that. And yet he recognized more and more that it was his thought, which was much more impressive in the original sound than if he had only dreamed this saying, for example, or had heard it from somewhere.

But he also felt an enlightening surprise regarding the flippancy and directness of the expression. No friend, no therapist could have told him so convincingly and unmaskingly that he considered his girlfriend a sex slave. Especially not a moralizer. Admittedly, the truth was also mocking, frivolous, a joke among men, but somehow it was also shameful. Above all, however, it belonged first of all only to him, and that made him happy, he found that really great. The fact that one can find the truth detector in oneself, he experienced like a small sensation. It is not easy to tell this to anyone else, nothing is better than when it is told to you - vice versa - by the therapist or by the Other in yourself.

He felt strongly motivated to continue with the exercises. But he also confessed this kind of truth to his girlfriend soon after, after which they both took a lot of time to talk about their relationship. Had he always seen her only like this? Could they talk openly about fantasies each had regarding their connection? How often do you just not come up with the right word, the right way to start a conversation? One must call the truth-detector in oneself, but this does not go in the usual way of an intention or a too blatant revelation that one does not trust oneself. If one can relate a dream when the other person knows how to interpret it, this may be a similarly good entry into deeper and honest communication. But who can do this? Even the therapist often needs to have heard whole series of dreams to be able to give an accurate interpretation.

On the other hand, the *pass-words*, which are set in motion by the breaking down structure of the *formula-word*s, are an ideal impetus for self-practice, self-analysis, and expanded communication. They have to do with the linguistics of the lie, but also that of the truth. That she "has always had her work clothes", with this my subject uncovered the lie that women like to work in these clothes. After all, everything is already there, the girlfriend only needs to get started. My subject knew very well that this was not right, but he had not grasped it. Even in the unconscious we know everything, even in sleep we sometimes know that we are dreaming, and even if we have understood this knowledge, we still have not grasped it. In the *pass-words* we do not always understand the meaning exactly, but they help us to grasp it, if one honestly adds a few expanding thoughts.

This immediacy of confrontation with truth does not occur in the Freudian "feeling of happiness at the satisfaction of a wild drive untamed by the ego", that is, a body-related enjoyment. Precisely this also falls away with substitute satisfactions and tamed, 'goal-inhibited' drive satisfactions and the untamed can thus never and nowhere be directly realized, because the human constitution, social rules and cultural achievements stand in the way as Freud explained. So the truth has to be found in another way.

In the *Analytic Psychocatharsis*, however, such a not physical but body-related enjoyment exists, the catharsis namely, which satisfies the drive quite 'the other way around' and also contributes to the truth. Increased by self-sublimation, the drive excitation namely finds a direct way into the area which Freud calls "perceptual identity", thus the most primordial area of the psychic, this time - thus in the case of the *pass-word* - however not only in the form of a hallucination of an underlying desire, thus also of a kind of satisfaction of the unrestrained (of a *Rays*), but of a pausing enjoyment which can also speak (of a *Speaks*).

This '*Speaks*' is freed from proximity to psychosis because it is subject to the "guardian of our mental health", the 'censorship' that is operative even in sleep and emanates from something located between id-resistance, ego, and superego. The 'censorship' prevents us from waking up in the morning as a completely different person than the one we went to bed as at night. And so, even in the half-awake state of meditation, it helps to prevent thoughts other than *formula-words* from constantly taking over, if practiced consistently - perhaps with small intervals. Only in the short moments in which the censor nevertheless gives way a little, commonplace thoughts but also the *pass-words* come to light, which one can rationally discard for a short time, or take up as interesting after all and keep them.

Or one falls asleep, also this can happen, because the censor does not sleep, it serves the monitoring of the sleep. After discarding a *pass-word*, the *formula-words* are immediately practiced again, and thus no pathological phenomenon can arise. However, if one wants to utilize the *pass-word*, one ends the meditation. The enjoyment, which can also speak, is closely connected with the catharsis, because only in this way it is also possible to understand why the split can be overcome by it. The two exercises of *Analytic Psychocatharsis* may initially appear to be separate exercises, but after some time of practice they merge into one another.

The first exercise then leads via the cathartic path to the after-inside hearing, indeed often automatically to the *pass-word*. For in the 'shivering through' a new kind of body perception is reached, the flight, often even over-flight of the cathartic enjoyment, from which the second exercise gets its momentum. This is precisely the difference to conventional psychoanalysis, which can only realize this height through intellectuality and insight. If the split would only be shifted into other areas, there would be no sense.

7. Prometheus

One last time on the subject of life in the face of death. Because - to say it once again in conclusion - it is about this not only with Sisyphus, but also in the situations of today's existence, and that is good. One must be able to feel death and also to push it aside again, as Lacan says of the "l'homelette" (from homme, man, and omelette), the lamellar 'undead object' of the Freudian libido. Because the libido is not a psychic energy, but the eroticized *Rays/Speaks*, that projects far beyond the body like an protruding omelette. I explain this 'l'homelette', the 'undead object' for the time being again as the joining of the mirror and echo point in the nervous system, but also in the unconscious. Especially from the imaginary, which in meditation brings an expansion of space, I see the unconscious as something overlapping the brain functions like a 'l'homelette'. Is it the feeling of the heart or the gaze of the visual (visual cortex in the occipital lobe of the brain) that makes this experience of contact between the neurological and the psychic possible?

The Freudian libido can also be asexual, it is poorly explained by the term energy. It can stir, can be a writhing *Rays*, a shifting in and out of body images, and is more reminiscent of the fluid called 'prana' in Indian yoga. In the early phase of childhood development, the adolescent remains in such an imaginary-real state, which first represents largely uncontrolled psychic. In the first exercise of *Analytic Psychocatharsis* the lucid, bright and this liberating 'trickle through' to be an expression of this imaginary-real, this 'undead object' which is also a form of the *Rays*. It is not an organized living being, yet it is fluid, rhythmic, unconsciously psychic, and to that extent not dead. But it has object character, one can make concrete statements about it, and psychoanalysis lives from this.

With this concept of 'l'homelette' one can well explain psychosomatic illnesses, headaches, migraines, for example, because then the blood vessels in the head, which are sensitive to pain (the brain itself is insensitive to pain), are superimposed by what is wound out of mental conflicts into other parts of the body. One can also explain Sisyphus stone with it, because is not this an 'undead object'? Finally he, it, trolls down again from the summit, and perhaps Sisyphus is seen in this way a rheumatic who drags his pain up and down with him, or an overweight person who does the same with the too many pounds (in the first place, however, I believe as described in the initial text that it is the screwed-up libido with which he torments himself).

A very similar fate - and where some things come out even better as with Sisyphus - also Prometheus suffered. Many writers - including Camus again - have described Prometheus as the hero who brought to mankind the fire of true humane being, the fire of art, science and culture, but mankind today has fallen far behind again and so it is necessary to make a new attempt in this direction, Camus said. Like Sisyphus, Prometheus quarrelled with the gods, but was also part of their cosmos. "Today's humanity", writes A. Camus, "aspires only to the technical. It arrives at the outburst in its machines and considers art and its pretensions an obstacle . . „.

"By contrast, it is characteristic of Prometheus that he cannot separate the machine from art. He believes in the simultaneous liberation of the body and the soul . . . The myth of Prometheus reminds us . . that one serves man only when one serves him wholly [67]. . . . The longing for light", Camus now continues to write in a very personal way, has sent him, like Prometheus himself, to war, "I have joined the ranks marching before the open gates of hell . . . . Man is everywhere, everywhere his cry, his pain and his threat", and so for Camus, who must have enlisted in the army himself at the time, the path to light became hellish fire, which thus reminded him of Prometheus. But perhaps it was another kind of love lie than the one I described at the beginning.

For something of this kind occupied Camus for the rest of his life, namely the woman he married was a morphine addict and deceived him wherever possible. Did this result from the peculiar relationship Camus had with the other woman in his life, his mother, who was an al-

---

[67] Camus, A., in Mythos Prometheus, Reclam Verlag (1995) S. 144-47

most mute, about four hundred words mastered, mentally disturbed illiterate. "Camus revered her like a saint, although he describes her as inaccessible, even dismissive, apathetic, and resigned to fate. The mother", says I. Radisch, "stands at the beginning and at the end of his path. (...) The mother is the standard that Camus applied to the world".[68] Sandwiched between these extraordinary women, Camus needed his ancient heroes.

"But the myths do not live from themselves. They wait for us to embody them", and so Camus turns back to the positive side of his hero. "The bound hero, in the midst of lightning and divine thunder, preserves his calm faith in man. And so he is harder than the rock and more patient than the eagle", Camus writes in conclusion. His interpretation of the Prometheus myth is actually more on the level of an imaginary-real description than on sober linguistic symbolism. Thus I find that the Prometheus myth, like that of Sisyphus, is closer to *Analytic Psychocatharsis* than to psychoanalysis. For the more meditative is also about saving the machines and the art, body and mind, together, after having had a glimpse of hell.[69]

---

[68] Radisch, I., Camus: Das Ideal der Einfachheit - Eine Biographie (The Ideal of Simpicissity – a boigraphy), Rowohlt (2014)

[69] The first glimpse of darkness while sitting in meditation is always something not quite at home, but it clears quickly if you use a clear, psychoanalytically validated method.

As is known, Prometheus, who belongs to the Titans, is said to have deceived Zeus by assigning the bad pieces to Zeus and the good pieces to man at the animal sacrifice. Zeus then refused to let man possess the fire, but Prometheus stole it from him to bring it to the mankind. In return, however, he was forged to a rock in the Caucasus, where an eagle came daily to feed on his liver. But the ancient Greeks already knew that the liver is the organ that regenerates best. Removing half the liver, for example because of metastases in the case of cancer, is therefore no problem for today's surgeons.

If Freud has not written anything about Sisyphus, he has briefly spoken about Prometheus. However, he says something diametrically different from Camus and most other authors. He writes that the psychoanalytical material on the figure of Prometheus is incomplete, but at least allows a - fantastic sounding - conjecture about the origin of this human feat. Concerning the confrontation of early man with fire, he says, it looks "as if primitive man had been accustomed, when he encountered fire, to satisfy an infantile lust for it by extinguishing it through his urine stream".[70] Typicly man, so to speak. But probably also typical Freud, one might add.

"There can be no doubt about the original phallic conception of the lambent flame stretching upwards, according to existing legends", Freud continued to write. "The

---

[70] Freud, S., GW, Bd. XIV, S. 449

extinguishing of fire by urination . . . was thus like a sexual act with a man, a pleasure of male potency in homosexual competition. He who first renounced this pleasure, sparing the fire, could carry it away with him and force it into his service. By dampening the fire of his own sexual excitement, early man had thus tamed the natural power of fire. So this great cultural conquest would be the reward for a renunciation of the instinct (drive). And further [it sounds like this], as if the woman had been ordered to be the guardian of the fire kept captive on the domestic hearth, because her anatomical build forbids her to give in to such a lust temptation. It is also remarkable how regularly the analytical experiences testify the connection of ambition, fire and urinary eroticism".

Certainly it behaves in such a way that not a primitive man stole fire from gods, as it is said in the myth, but it was probably a question of how the first people tamed and managed the fire in forest or steppe caused by lightning. It must have actually seemed to them as a dramatic event sent from heaven, until they learned to maneuver it - barefoot and without equipment - out of a conflagration or blaze somewhat and then keep it alive in a hollow or elsewhere with combustible material in a limited way. It may well be that people, and here especially men, later, when the flames were well under control, noticed that the burning of the flames and that of the urethra when urinating were the same sensation, the equally felt event.

But does this still have something to do with the essence of Prometheus?

Freud thinks: yes, because the myth says that Prometheus brought the stolen embers of fire to earth hidden in the 'cavity' of an oversized 'fennel tube'. Although Freud concedes that the word 'cavity' interferes with his interpretation of the tube as a pure phallic symbol, there would be a form often typical of the dream, namely the "transformation into the opposite", so that it is about the water of the urine stream, which is transported in the tube and with which the fire can be extinguished. And further: the fire theft must be punished, here, however, in psychoanalytic point of view, in a "fire extinguishing abnegation"![71] This fun, to enjoy the emptying of the urethra, belongs to be forbidden, states the psychoanalyst Freud, inserting from the 'divine prerogative' (which must be preserved by punishment) the modern superego.

I think it is like Sisyphus here about two different things. Sisyphus dies twice and lives on (as a sun-nature, as a hero, as a hard worker) but somehow also twice. Prometheus stands for the bringer and tamer of the fiery burning inside as well as outside, because Freud is right that early humans closely connected "mental processes with physical expressions". Everything was somehow bodily animated, physically animated, fiery and libidinous burning were not always completely separable (I re-

---

[71] Freud, S., GW Bd. XVI, S. 5

member the "inner touch" of Heller-Roazen, this 'Koenesthesia', i.e. the jointly, namely inside and outside sensed).[72] It is about an eroticized all unifying feeling, is it perhaps that which has brought Prometheus?

But then, of course, one can also imagine other correlations, where it did not just burn in the urethra, but also in hands and feet, in heart and brain. The libido also has correspondences inside one's own body. In the context of primary narcissistic development, a kind of direct mirroring self-love, it may yet have more to do with the visual, with the feelers of the look, the gaze, than with the guttering in the urethra. Freud himself reported that "it would be as if the unconscious, by means of the system perception-consciousness [i.e., an unconscious gaze], extended feelers to the external world, which were quickly withdrawn after tasting its excitations".[73]

According to this, it is rather a burning in the visual system, in the bodily images, which again reminds of the 'trickling through', of the Id *Rays*, which is more glistening than burning, but this is, after all, particularly typical for the unconscious. It is, after all, the focal point of the brain concave mirror, the mirror point of the *Rays*, which is significant in psychoanalysis and meditation. Also Lucifer, the Light-Fire-Binger in the monotheistic uni-

---

[72] Heller-Roazen, D., Der innere Sinn: Archäologie eines Gefühls ((The Inner Touch, archeology of an inner feeling), fischer wissenschaft (2012)

[73] Freud, S., GW XIII, S. 387-91

verse has not been noticed primarily by his 'urethral ambition', as much as this term has its significance in the psychoanalytic treatment situation.

As said, Freud's concept of libido has its justification for myth, for psychoanalysis, but also for *Analytic Psychocatharsis*. Libido is as much "longing for light" and "hellish fire" as Camus thematizes it. Undoubtedly, the light-fire-bringer has always something pathological about it, which is no longer connected with punishment as in myth or with warning against the devil's work in religion. But it is still not unproblematic today, even if we tolerate all libidinous extravagances and gender freedoms today, it can often go wrong with too much. It is not for nothing that Lacan calls sex an illusory relationship, for it is not only the appearance of it all, but also the glaring appearance of lust, the 'light', the 'fire' that is involved. Also the show, the eroticized look, the covert forms of voyeurism and exhibitionism of every one, belongs to it.

Tolerating does not mean recognizing gender freedoms in the fullest and most constructive sense. In a cardiovascular rehab clinic where I worked for a year, heart patients were always told they'd better masturbate if the sexual tension became too much. In other words, a 'urethral discharge' was never all bad, was relaxing. For the 'Kurschatten' ('cure shadow', what in German ment a ladie friend met during a stay at a spa) was not the right help. In a ten-year statistic of this clinic, a so-called 'love death' was found fourteen times, which occurred only once with the visiting wife, but mainly with other women who were themselves in rehab. Apparently, the tension with a woman other than the one being married is significantly higher and so is the risk of another infarction. But I didn't find the recommendation for masturbation very appropriate either. Lacan said that masturbation is the enjoyment of the idiot, after all it takes place with a photo or only with a fantasy and not with a living and original other.

But what is really true about Prometheus? I also worked in a mental hospital for another year and subsequently cared for a patient for almost twenty years. He wrote poems and texts, which I published in a book together with the course of therapy.[74] One of these texts is about Prometheus, but more in the direction of Camus again, maybe my patient even took some things from him, because it sounds similar.

"I had hoped to meet Prometheus, who knows my pain, the density that makes me solid. Prometheus was chained to his firmness, to that which is tangibly dense. We are chained to our thoughts, naked as Prometheus to the hardness of his rock, which is the measure of the soul. I don't like this world where nothing is right, I don't like the people who go along with it all soul-quiet. I don't

---

[74] Hummel, von, G., Das Gerade und das Gekrümmte (The Straight and the Warped), BoD (2012)

like the painless ones who are always victorious, nor the excited, upset ones who are always on top. I don't like life. We are like Prometheus a bit above it all, like the first great man".

I see Prometheus awaiting his eagle, lovingly, impatiently, who will bring him relief, regeneration. 'When will you come again to feed from me', he calls after him, for the liver does not hurt. `When will you come again`? 'Tomorrow`. Again and again there will be a tomorrow. The glances will meet without making a picture. As A. Gide said, "Prometheus is badly tied up", his eagle is nothing but his love for his own shadow. And so Prometheus calls him again and again: "Come again and bring at last the image of freedom, I can stand my pain"! One day Prometheus shook off his chains (supposedly Heracles would have freed him), took his eagle and lived where he wanted, pure".

My patient was really a pain patient, sometimes suffering from facial neuralgia, perhaps also from the treatments with neuroleptics. But the pain-loving, masochistic Prometheus cannot be his salvation, I thought to myself. In my view, Prometheus is the socialist who clearly loved people more than his fellow god. But to the right-wing populist dictator Zeus, the social aids of his original party comrade are a thorn in his side. As so often, the socialists are equated with the weak and neurotic spirits. In neurosis the fear-pleasure prevails, writes the psychoanalyst M. Balint, and such a bit of neuroticism could be suspected in the constant thief Prometheus.[75] Stealing is a form of anxiety-pleasure par excellence.

But I let my patient go on talking and writing. *"I see the terrible things, wars, child labor, exploitation, psychic annihilation, can one still be without pain? Prometheus only says to his eagle: these principles, regulations, laws, privileges, all these gods I disregard. Not a career, not a top manager, not one of those top people who play Olympus. No, Prometheus doesn't want to stay among the chic, among the media-hungry celebrities, and so he snuggles up to the pyritic skin of his rock, warms himself on its veins of copper oxide and mica. The branching of fine granite traces, amethyst crystal, rhombic runes listening and speaking to him: Consolation, homage, as long as you remain faithful to me in firmness, you will remain an important deed, and will be a salvation for others".*

Sisyphus, Prometheus and many other mythical or otherwise exemplary figures, they all make human relationships clearer to us, but ultimately not clear enough. With the ancient Greek heroes there are always so many possible interpretations, and with the great poets and philosophers it is really no different. Also scientists do not become prophets valid forever in spite of their accuracy and knowledge. Their research results are not refuted,

---

[75] Balint, M., Angstlust und Regression (Anxiety-pleasure and Regression), Rowohlt (1972)

but they become special cases, which become more and more insignificant in the context of the totality of a science. This is also criticized by the philosopher of science H. Hastedt when he writes that "the mind in the participant perspective as subject of cognition is methodically prior to mind and body as objects of cognition in the observer perspective.[76] What will always retain its value, therefore, is each individual's journey inward, to the central subject point, to the id as the other of each self.

It is not who dies sooner who is dead longer, but who dies better really knows what is at stake in the confrontation with the absolute end. This is the lesson of Sisyphus, Prometheus and many other poems. To die well is to live not better, but properly, and to do so with a trained regression, with an assured looking back, indeed a 'living back and dying forward'. A life without such a reassurance, that is, without a reinforcement from backward for a final forward, has little sense. After all, it is necessary, if one day one simply doesn't want anymore, if it has to run by itself, if there is therefore an absolute end that one can then die forward.

To die forward shall not mean to die again into a new life, but into the very last sense of life, which must come well, freely, creatively - as I wrote it in the beginning - by itself (especially by the *pass-words*). This 'from-itself', of course, one must be able to perceive as the gift

---

[76] Hastedt, H., Das Leib-Seele Problem (The Life-Soul problem), Suhrkamp 1989) S. 291

of the unconscious. Inferiority complexes and the 'nothing-more-being' of the aging person block this view. Then it is good - as Sisyphus did - to come to terms with death, which after all is nothing else but also a side of the other in the unconscious and whose answers are always *pass-word* just.

To say that one should talk to death would sound as too direct, too sweeping and almost paradoxical, because nowadays we don't see him as a person who unexpectedly knocks on the door dressed in black. But to see him as the side of the negation of the Other gives him a psychoanalytically proven form, in that this, this Other is a "mirror in which the true of the gaze is founded" (Lacan, Seminar XVII). This is true insofar as a speaking also participates on that (one could say: the word in its broken form), which is the point of finding identity, in which death is always in the background.

For without death in the background, one knows nothing of the truth of life. But I do not want to proclaim philosophical doctrines here. One can have these everywhere from somewhere else. One must look into this conundrum-mirror of one's own identity itself, where it shows itself best in the form of the *Rays* (first exercise) and the form of the *Speaks* (second exercise). There is no getting around concrete practice. "All theory is grey", said Goethe, "and the golden tree of life is green". In this way, one can also gild one's death. I briefly describe how this practice works in the appendix.

Sisyphus, Prometheus and many other mythical or otherwise exemplary figures, they all make human relationships clearer to us, but ultimately not clear enough. With the ancient Greek heroes there are always so many possible interpretations, and with the great poets and philosophers it is really no different. Also scientists do not become prophets valid forever in spite of their accuracy and knowledge. Their research results are not refuted, but they become special cases, which become more and more insignificant in the context of the totality of a science. This is also criticized by the philosopher of science H. Hastedt when he writes that "the mind in the participant perspective as subject of cognition is methodically prior to mind and body as objects of cognition in the observer perspective. What will always retain its value, therefore, is each individual's journey inward, to the central subject point, to the id as the other of each self.

It is not who dies sooner who is dead longer, but who dies better really knows what is at stake in the confrontation with the absolute end. This is the lesson of Sisyphus, Prometheus and many other poems. To die well is to live not better, but properly, and to do so with a trained regression, with an assured looking back, indeed a 'living back and dying forward'. A life without such a reassurance, that is, without a reinforcement from backward for a final forward, has little sense. After all, it is necessary, if one day one simply doesn't want anymore, if it has to run by itself, if there is therefore an absolute end that one can then die forward.

To die forward shall not mean to die again into a new life, but into the very last sense of life, which must come well, freely, creatively - as I wrote it in the beginning - by itself (especially by the *pass-words*). This 'from-itself', of course, one must be able to perceive as the gift of the unconscious. Inferiority complexes and the 'nothing-more-being' of the aging person block this view. Then it is good - as Sisyphus did - to come to terms with death, which after all is nothing else but also a side of the other in the unconscious and whose answers are always *pass-word* just.

In the *Analytic Psychocatharsis* the 'true of the gaze' is prepared, pre-paved in the cathartic liberation of the first exercise. It acts like a merging, blending experience of short duration, which is based on an elementary assimilation longing, a merging imagination with the primary mirror, which *Rays* in the depth of every human being. To satisfy the phantasm of fusion or merging alone is of little value, indeed, it can become the basis of neurosis or is even completely impossible. Therefore, in the second exercise, the 'true of the mirror gaze' must be crowned by an interpretation, a *pass-word*. But even this is perhaps not the last goal that is reached in the dying life, in this last phase described by N. Sestan. There and only there the phantasm of fusion is really fulfilled.

That and only that is the meaning of this twice dying, the one that the doctors determine with great medical technology, and the other that still waits for the fusion experience or realization or however one may say it, before everything is really over. In such a way and only in such a way, if this intermediate phase is still - yes what? experienced, wandered through,? no word fits - one can die happily.

I do not want to proclaim philosophical doctrines here. The fact that one does not know anything of the truth of life without the death in the background, one can have everywhere from somewhere else. In this regard, one must also discuss the question of assisted suicide. It is increasingly placed in the hands of the suicide-willing themselves. It is not uncommon to find someone who is not suffering from a serious, incurable disease but nevertheless wishes to die prematurely. Suicide, of course, prevents one from still experiencing and enjoying the intermediate realm of life while dying, at least one should know that.

It is better to still look into this conundrum mirror of one's own identity at the usual time of life itself, where it is shows best in the *Rays*-form (first exercise) and *Speaks*-form (second exercise) of *Analytic Psychocatharsis* and where the best pre-understanding for this last phase of life can be achieved.. There is no getting around concrete practice. "All theory is grey", said Goethe, "and the golden tree of life is green". In this way, one can also gild one's death. I briefly describe how this practice works - of which an ounce is more important than a ton of theory - in the appendix.

Appendix

The procedure of *Analytic Psychocatharsis* is very simple from its practical side - as already described in part.
Nevertheless, I will give here a short summary and further *formula-words*.[77] You sit in a comfortable posture
and repeat one, two or up to five *formula-words* slowly
one after the other purely in your mind, while at the
same time you pay attention to whether something appears that has the character of an 'Id *Rays*'. The "ray" can
be an enlightenment, body image perception, a shimmer,
a 'spot of light', or a basic lucidity that is associated with
such a phenomenon. So the ray is not something one has
to imagine, create or even force oneself. It is present in
every human being as the primary form of a drive
(sopic-drive) and thus only has to be awakened or expected. In the same way, a 'trickling through' can also be
felt or the sensation can emerge how one's own body
image shifts,[78] widens or is simply fixed as black paint,

---

[77] Further formula words can be found in other publications
or on the website given below. For the time being, these are
sufficient. You should not need more than five.

[78] This is an experience that has something to do with atavistic emotional reactions. The early humans still felt a lot with
their uncovered skin, touched it and communicated in an
environment-related way. Even with moving pieces of music,
when it grips you like a shiver trickling down your back, we
fall back on these particularly deep emotions. In *Analytic
Psychocatharsis*, however, this experience is used as confir-
mation of an insight, e.g. in the *pass-words*.

as a stain in front of the closed eyes. Because black is already a perception, which can stand out from the darkness in the head quite slightly. No matter what is 'seen' or 'experienced', it will have the character of even a very small 'Id *Rays*', and that is enough.

Thus a relaxation occurs, a catharsis, a liberation experience, which can be increased especially if at the same time the said *formula-words* are practiced purely mentally. At the bottom left one can see a different Formula-Word as I have given in the main text. Also this (RADIC-IT) is not a normal word from Latin, but it contains several overlapping meanings in one formulation, it is 'linguistically crystalline' like Lacan said from the unconscious. Besides the radiat and dicit (*Rays* and *Speaks*) there are several disparate meanings written in a circle and read from different letters. For example, here one can also use "adi cit r" (approach, it moves R), "C i tradi" (handed over a hundred i), "citra di" (on this side the gods), "dicit ra" (it says ra), "r adic it" (add r, it goes), "radi cit" (get scratched, it moves),

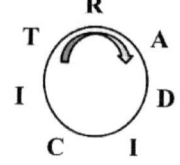

"trad ici" (tell, I have met) etc., whereby much sounds quite absurd. But this has no meaning for the formal expression. It is only decisive to be able to clearly explain the scientific reasoning (several meanings in one formulation, use only of other interfaces), and this is very important for the procedure, because this is the only way to have full confidence in the method.

This is the first exercise which is based on actual guide-lines of psychoanalysis, because mental reverberation generates a regression (an inner retreat) which at the same time concentrates only on a narrowed aspect of the looking drive, the perceptual instinct (the *Rays*). In addition, *formula-word* repetition takes the place of what in psychoanalysis is called the obligation to repeat, the unconscious repetition. This is at least abolished as long as the exercises of the *Analytic Psychocatharsis* are effective. I have already indicated in the main text that this simplifies and reduces an essential hurdle of classical psychoanalysis. It is important that it comes to a catharsis, to a liberation experience and not only to a simple relaxation. At least for some time one frees oneself from the unconscious obligation to repeat.

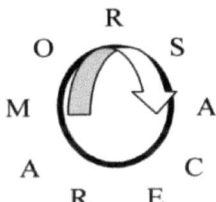

As far as other forms of therapy and their problems are concerned, by using *Analytic Psychocathar-sis* it is usually possible to avoid them in a simplified way. It is no longer enough simply to believe a therapist or meditation teacher and follow his simple instructions. Nowadays it is also necessary to understand that the method has a scientific basis and that one can and should participate with own thoughts. This way, in deeper moments of the exercises dependencies on the ideology of the method, on the teacher or therapist or irrational fears do not occur. The Id *Rays* (crystalline) of the cathartic experience are thus derived from the basic power of the scopic drive. It is therefore something that is originally present in every human being, just like the Id *Speaks* (the linguistic, the uttering).[79]

After the R-A-D-I-C-I-T, the *formula-word* O-R-S-A-C-E-R-A-M can be added, because if someone is really interested in learning the analytic pychocathartic method, at least three of these formulations are necessary. Two or even just one would tire one out too quickly. In the *formula-word* C-E-R-A-M-O-R-S-A (picture previous page) - once written differently - there are following meanings depending on initial letter: C eram orsa (I was a hundred times beginning, amo R sacer (I love the holy R), cera morsa (the fragmented wax), mors acer (death is bitter), amor sacer (love is holy), etc.). How to emphasize, one can forget these meanings immediately again. They are too disparate, i.e. cannot be reduced to any denominator. For if one practices them in the uniform lettering, one will never bring together the bitter death with the fragmented wax and the hundredfold beginning in one meaning. It is only important to understand how the *formula-words* are structured, so that one can scientifically-intellectually question the process of any time.

---

[79] In psychoanalysis we assume that symbolic order or language plays a decisive role in human development, dividing perception into a pure sensory activity and a drive activity. The activity of the senses is a real perception, the activity of instinct a pleasure of perception, in summary we speak of perceptiveness. The true comes in through language (Id *Speaks*), the perception through reality (Id *Rays*).

If any feelings or ideas arise that are inappropriate or frightening, one can reflect or read more about the process. Blind faith is not required.

In the second exercise, attention is now paid to exactly this *Speaks*, this body echo, i.e. to a sound coming from above / right in the head, to a tone, sound, from the deep inside. After all, these are letters that emanate from this 'typographic' space and which the unconscious holds stored there. And it is precisely into this space that the *formula-words* have penetrated and have awakened and evoked the letters in their 'B(r)uchstaben'-likeness (broken-letterings). Again, the same applies here: it is a completely original aspect of the drive to express or speak, which is present in every human being as a primary process and even takes on the form of very brief, compact "inner sentences", "ultra-reduced phrases" in the unconscious (all concepts of Lacan for this phonetic experience).

Here, too, at first only a fine noise, a distant sound or similar can be perceived, but the practitioner will notice from the beginning that this is a concentration on a more up-right or up-central hearing system in the head. The echoes of the body have a relationship to this, which is being referred to here. Even if the actual hearing and speech system in the head is left-handed, the more rudimentary, musical and more regression accessible hearing and speech system are present on the right side and its echo structure is clearly recognizable. The short phrases of the *pass-words* are more suitable for this, while the left-sided system (psychoanalytically: the preconscious) plays a role in the longer ones.

If you read something about psychoanalysis and keep in touch with literary, scientific and other cultures, and have also read the present text, made an attempt with the exercises, in short: if you are a bit of an educated citizen, you will interpret the often immediately visible *pass-words* correctly. Thus Freud writes that even some dreams, which are now much more distorted than the *pass-words*, and which come directly from the symbolic-real, could be read directly from the "sheet". It is no longer necessary to ask the dreamer about his ideas and to bring in cumbersome interpretations.

And one last hint, which is often asked for. If one notices during the application of *Analytic Psychocatharsis* that the Id *Rays* portion during practice is too strong, one switches to the Id *Speaks* exercise and vice versa. Otherwise, both exercises should only be performed for about twenty minutes. The change between practical experience and theoretical thinking is important because in the end something in common will emerge: a mental self-awareness, a practical logic, a cathartic analysis. In the end, both exercises find their way to an inner 'mission', to a certainty of 'What's about the ONE',[80] and thus

---

[80] This concerns the title of my book, also published in English, which deals with the same subject by means of literature and mathematics.

to the possibility of being able to participate in the procedure.

On the other hand, I have already described that sometimes one does not only deviate from the meditative process in thoughts. Sometimes one even deviates between the individual *formula-words* to images, memories, to a mixture of both and to *pass-words*, and yet returns to *formula-word* reversion. The advanced student will experience this as enriching, because he does not allow himself to be seduced into a one-sided direction of radiation or speech, but remains in the progression in the narrow combination of the two basic drives, basic principles, mirroring- and echo-discourse.

Examples of these *pass-words* I have described several in the text. Everybody has to be patient and try out what he thinks is a safe word can. Sometimes it's like you're almost in retrospect, in the final phase of the *pass-word* experience, the phrase-hearing the short sentence. Sometimes it seems it's a very, very quiet thought, but still is clear or quite clear. I have to be so vague here, nevertheless there is no doubt about the phenomenon both from the psychoanalytic theory as well as from the many experiences I have had to collect. Even if the actual hearing-talking system in the head is left-sided is laid out, the more rudimentary is on the right side, musical and the regression more accessible auditory Intercom system available.

Again: After the first exercise, the mental repetition of several *formula-words* with a simultaneous occurrence thereof see if you have a ray, a lucidity, a trickle, a liberating, cathartic experience, you move on to the second exercise. Here you concentrate to the sound, the tone, the *Speaks* from above or right inside until you have completely transcended body-consciousness has. If you notice that the ray portion of the training is too much is strong, you switch to the Speech Exercise and vice versa. Each exercise should be performed for about twenty minutes.

The aim of the procedure is to achieve an ideal, successful and satisfying combination of the two exercises. I cannot make any definite specifications here, because when the Ray and *Speaks* exercises, are fulfilling in their combination, everyone should be able to know for himself. After all, the experiences mature in progress with the theory, about which one can read oneself or justify it oneself. The change between practical experience and theoretical thinking is important because in the end something in common will emerge: a mental self-awareness, a practical logic, a cathartic analysis. Ultimately, both exercises can also lead to an inner 'assignment', to a certainty of being able to participate in the shaping of the procedure.

For just as Freud spoke of 'lay analysis' because he did not want to have only academics in his ranks, the argument that the procedure should not depend on professions and titles is even more valid for Analytical Psychocatharsis. To this day, analysts worldwide are only physicians and psychologists with university training. Here, the father of psychoanalysis has not been followed, although such a following is required in the essential points. But one can become a scientist also outside the university, which would also help to make the scholastic, university discourse really an analytic discourse.

Website of the Author: analytic-psychocatharsis.com
where one can also find several articles in English about
psychoanalysis and the method of *Analytical Psychocatharsis*.

Bibliography

Baggini, J., Ich denke, also will ich, (I think, so I want) dtv (2016)

Barkhaus, A., Mayer, M., Identität, Leiblichkeit, Normativität (identity, corporeality, normativity (Suhrkamp (1996)

Bauriedl, T., Beziehungsanalyse, (relationship analysis) Suhrkamp (1993)

Benthien, C., Wulf, Ch., Körperteile (body parts), Rowohlt (2001)

Bezzel, C., Wittgenstein, Junius (1996)

Breuer, R., Immer Ärger mit dem Urknall (Always Trouble with the Big Bang), Rowohlt (1993)

Brockman, J., Vogel, S., Wie funktioniert die Welt? (How does the world work), Fischer Taschenbuch (2013)

Byung-Chul Han, Die Austreibung des Anderen (The Expulsion of the Other), Fischer Wissenschaft (201)

Byung-Chul Han, Die Errettung des Schönen (The Salvation of Beauty), Fischer Wissenschaft (201)

Camus, A., Der Mythos des Sisyphos, Rowohlt (2018)

Carnap, R., Einführung in die Philosophie der Naturwissenschaft (Introduction to the Philosophy of Natural Science) (1969)

Damasio, A. R., Descartes` Irrtum, Dtv (1997)

Dennet, D. C., Von den Bakterien zu Bach – und zurück, Suhrkamp (2018)

Davies, P., Gott und die moderne Physik (God and modern physics), Bert. M. (1986)

Eccles, J. C., Gehirn und Seele, Piper (1987)

Eichmeier, J., Höfer, O., Endogene Bildmuster, U&S – Verlag (1974)

Fischer-Lichte, E., Performativität: Eine Einführung, transcript (2012)

Freud, S., Studienausgabe, Fischer (1989)

Goel, B. S. Meditation und Psychoanalyse, Ariston (1989)

Görz, G., Einführung in die Künstliche Intelligenz (Introduction to Artificial Intelligence), Addison-Wesley (1996)

Harari, Y. N., Homo Deus, C. H. Beck (2017)

Heidegger, M., Unterwegs zur Sprache, G. Neske (1959)

Hilbrecht, H., Meditation und Gehirn, Schattauer (2010)

Hofstadter, D., Die Analogie, Klett-Cotta (2014)

Horgan, J., An den Grenzen des Wissens, Luchterhand (1997)

Hustvedt, S., Die gleissende Welt (The blazing Wiorld) Rowohlt (2016)

Husttvedt, S., Das Leiden eines Amerikanmers, Rowohlt (2009)

Hustvedt, S., Wenn Gefühle auf Worte treffen (When feelings meet words) , Kampa (2019)

Jacobs, A., Schrott, R., Gehirn und Gedicht, Hanser (2011

Jakobson, R., Semiotik, Suhrkamp (1988)

Jakobson, R., On Language, Harvard University Press (1995)

Jung. C.G., Gesammelte Werke, Walter (1983)

Kant, I., Kritik der reinen Vernunft, Reclam (1966)

Kluge, F., Etymologisches Wörterbuch, W. de Gruyter (1989)

Lacan, J., Schriften I - III, Walter, (1975)

Lacan, J., Seminare I,I, VII, XI, XX, Quadriga (1980-1995)

Lacan, J., Seminaire Nr. III, Iv, VIII, XVII, Edition Seuil (1981-1994)

Lacan, J., Die Bildungen des Unbewussten, Turia & Kant (2006)

Lacan, J., Mitschriften der Seminare,VI,IX,X,XII,XV, B.R.L.F., Strasbourg

Laplanche, J., Pontalis, J. B., Das Vokabular Der Psychoanalyse, Suhrkamp (1989)

Linke, D., Kunst und Gehirn, Rowohlt (2001)

Maar, C., Pöppel, E., Christaller, T., Die Technik auf dem Weg zur Seele, Rowohlt (1996)

Merleau-Ponty, M., Das Sichtbare und das Unsichtbare (The Visible and the Invisible) Fink Verlag (1994)

Pinker, S., Der Sprachinstinkt, Kindler (1996)

Plato, Sämtliche Werke, Insel Verlag (1991)

Popper, K. R., Eccles, J. C., Das Ich und sein Gehirn, Piper (1989)

Potthoff, P., Die Begegnung der Subjekte (The Encounter of Subjects), Psychosozial-Verlag (2014)

Roazen, D., Der innere Sinn, Archäologie eines Gefühls (The Inner Touch, Archaeology of Feeling), Fischer (2012)

Roheim, G., Die Panik der Götter (The Panic of the Gods), Kindler (1975)

Rosset, C., Das Reale in seiner Einzigartigkeit (The real in its uniqueness), Merve (2000)

Rüdinger, D., Perrez, M., Anthropologische Aspekte der Psychologie, O. Müller (1979)

Rudgley, R., Abenteuer Steinzeit (Adventure Stoneage), Kremaye & Scheriau (2001)

Schmidt-Hellerau, C., Lebenstrieb & Todestrieb (Life Drive & Death Drive), Libido & Lethe, Verlag Intern. Psychoanalyse (1995)

Searle, J. R., Geist, Hirn und Wissenschaft, Suhrkamp (1992)

Seidler, G. H., Der Blick des Anderen (The View of the Other), Verlag Intern, Psychoanalyse (1995)

Sinz, R., Gehirn und Gedächtnis, Fischer Utb (1981)

Strowik, E., Sprechende Körper (Speaking Bodies), Fink-Verlag (2009)

Thompson, R. F., Das Gehirn, Spectrum (1994)

Thorne, K. S., Gekrümmter Raum und Verbogene Zeit, Knaur (1996)

Tipler, F. J., Über die Omegapunkttheorie, Piper (1994)

Uexküll, Th., Fuchs, M., Subjektive Anatomie, Schattauer (1994)

Weiss, Der Andere in der Übertragung (The Other in Transference), Frommann-Holzboog, (1988)

Weizsäcker, C. F. von, Die Einheit der Natur (The Unity of Nature), Dtv (1995)

Weinberg, S., Der Traum von der Einheit des Universums, Bertelsmann (1993)

Weizenbaum, J., Die Macht der Computer, Stw (1977)

Wiener, O., Probleme der Künstlichen Intelligenz, Merve (1990)

Wilhelm, R., Informatik, C.H.Beck (1996)

Wilson, E. O., Der Wert der Vielfalt, Piper (199

Wolf, F. A., Die Physik der Träume, Byblos (1996)

Wygotski, L. S., Denken und 'Sprechen (Thinking and 'Speaking)', Fischer (1981)

Books published in English by the author

The physically sick Soul

In this booklet of only forty pages, the author describes in a simplified form the method of *Analytic Psychocatharsis* that he developed. It is not only about the mentally ill soul, but also about the treatment of the disorder expressed in a more physical form.

What about the ONE

The One is only insufficiently described in mathematics. It is about the spiritual-physical unity of man, which can only be achieved through a combination of psychoanalytical and meditative exercises. The author describes this process using the literature of Siri Hustvedt and other female authors as well as the psychoanalysis of J. Lacan.

The vertical Ego
A Path to self-analytical Practice
Günter von Hummel

The vertical Ego

Our usual social Ego is oriented horizontally, but the essential and still predominantly unconscious Ego is oriented in the vertical. This is connected with primary inner psychic reflections, which are not exactly captured by psychoanalysis, because it is more oriented to the word. With a few meditative exercises one can reach the sufficiently good vertical and unite it with the horizontal.

Further books by the author from MCS-Verlag in German

Analytic Psychocatharsis

Psychoanalytic theory and cathartic meditation cannot simply be transferred into each other. If, however, both methods are related by a decisive element (formula words containing several meanings in one stroke), a new method of one's own can be established. Psychoanalysis and meditative methods are discussed, and the practice of one's own procedure is described in detail.

The Revolt of the Self

The classical method of analysis of the unconscious represents a too theoretical revolt of the self. In order to be successful in practice, a more direct self-analytic procedure is required, which everyone can develop out of themselves. Formulations that contain several meanings in a single stroke of writing can break up the unconscious of each individual through mental practice and free him or herself.

'teadrunken' The starting point of the book is the doctrine of the psychoanalyst O. Earl Wittgenstein, who assumed that man contains three parts within himself, which he can only combine in different ways to form a unity or uniform personality. He calls the ultimate and ideal unity the 'trialogue'. On the basis of the description of several mountain climbs, the author roams through all possible cultural and psychological questions in order to achieve the 'trialogue' through hiking, meditation and intellectual

Yoga and Psychoanalysis
Based on a scientific biography of the religious scientist and yoga teacher Kirpal Singh (Surat Shand Yoga), all forms of yoga are compared from the perspective of psychoanalysis. It is necessary to establish a procedure of one's own, which the author also calls *Analytic Psychocatharsis*. Numerous pictures and diagrams make the book attractive.